SCOTTISH STEAM
1948-1967

PETER TUFFREY

GREAT N-ORTHERN

ACKNOWLEDGEMENTS

I am grateful for the help received from the following people: Roger Arnold, Ben Brooksbank, David Burrill, John Chalcraft, David Christie, John Clayson, D.J. Dippie, John Law, Hugh Parkin, Bill Reed, Andrew, Rachel and Sue Warnes, Tony Watson, Bill Wright.

Gratitude should also be expressed to my son Tristram for his general help and encouragement throughout the course of the project.

Great Northern Books
PO Box 1380, Bradford, BD5 5FB
www.greatnorthernbooks.co.uk

© Peter Tuffrey 2022

ISBN: 978-1-914227-21-9

Design and layout: David Burrill

CIP Data
A catalogue for this book is available from the British Library

INTRODUCTION

Comprising one-third of the land mass of mainland Britain, Scotland provided a diverse background for railway photographers to record the end of steam. As dieselisation radiated northward from Southern England, the country became a refuge for locomotives and many enthusiasts rushed with their cameras to record the demise of a great period in British history.

Like English counterparts, early railways in Scotland were developed for the movement of freight and minerals. One of the earliest undertakings was the Kilmarnock & Troon Railway, which was in fact a plateway, authorised in 1808 and ready for coal traffic during 1812. Initially using wooden rails, the upgrade to iron was made in 1815 and by the end of the decade, a steam locomotive – the first in Scotland – had been purchased. Passenger traffic had also begun shortly after the opening of the line.

The Monkland & Kirkintilloch Railway was another pioneer, being completed in 1826 to transport coal from collieries east of Glasgow to the Forth & Clyde Canal which connected the cities of Edinburgh and Glasgow. This broke the monopoly of the Monkland Canal and coal prices were reduced as a result, with the profits of the M&KR steadily increasing from opening to the 1830s.

As these early railways proved themselves, so did those in England (Liverpool & Manchester and Stockton & Darlington) and this gave investors the confidence to supply money for new schemes. The connection of Edinburgh and Glasgow by rail had been mooted in the early 1820s, yet the cost and risk involved deterred the project until the mid-1830s and work was authorised at the end of the decade. Costing over £1,000,000, the 46-mile-long line was completed in 1842 and ran from Queen Street, Glasgow, to Haymarket in Edinburgh. At the aforementioned end, the terminus could only be departed from using the steep Cowlairs incline which was necessary after strong opposition from the canal owners was shown to the competing railway interests.

Whilst many early railway schemes were local in nature, the continued success of longer, inter-city lines saw thoughts turned to connecting England with Scotland. Much of Northern England had early railway undertakings, meaning the cost and scope of such a project was not too overwhelming. Promoters of the Edinburgh & Glasgow Railway took the opportunity to extend along the East Coast to reach Berwick-upon-Tweed, where George Hudson had promised to meet the new line with one from Newcastle where a connection could be made with the wider system in England, eventually reaching London. In 1844, the line was authorised and work was completed within two years, though the Newcastle & Berwick line was not ready until the following year. The North British Railway was not the only company striving for a connection with England. The Caledonian Railway was formed in 1845 to link Glasgow

with the western side of England, aiming for Carlisle. This was also reached within two years and by 1850 two lines connected Edinburgh and Glasgow to England.

The 'Railway Mania' of the mid-1840s saw a number of lines proposed and some of these were constructed. Generally, these were locally focused and often ripe for takeover by the emerging larger companies – the North British Railway and Caledonian Railway. These were not completely dominant, however. The Glasgow, Paisley, Kilmarnock & Ayr Railway joined forces with another company that planned to connect with Carlisle and formed the Glasgow & South Western Railway in the process. This company went on to monopolise the area south west of Glasgow and prevented incursion of the CR, though a working relationship existed.

As the southern half of the country was connecting by rail, the task of linking the north to the growing network was occurring. The Edinburgh & Northern Railway reached Dundee in the late 1840s and in 1850 travel to Aberdeen was possible. Around this time, a project for a line from the latter to Inverness was underway, though construction did not start until 1852 and ready for traffic in 1854. This was done under the Great North of Scotland Railway and the company went on to be the dominant force in North East Scotland. Competition was later provided by the Highland Railway which was formed from the Inverness & Perth Junction Railway and Inverness & Aberdeen Junction Railway in 1865. The aforementioned was recently constructed to provide an alternative route to Highland traffic moving via Aberdeen and Dundee. The company's territory stretched into the far North of Scotland.

The Caledonian, North British, Glasgow & South Western, Great North of Scotland and Highland Railway companies went on to dominate Scottish rail traffic. This was primarily freight, particularly coal from the various coalfields, but also passengers moving around the country. After the First World War, the Government pondered on which direction to take going forward, having assumed responsibility for the railways during the conflict. There were some calls for Nationalisation to continue, though the political will to do so was lacking. The result was the formation of the 'Big Four' railway companies in the Grouping of 1923. In Scotland, this meant two companies were to absorb the above-mentioned: Caledonian, Glasgow & South Western and Highland Railways into the London Midland & Scottish Railway; North British and Great North of Scotland Railways formed part of the London & North Eastern Railway. The two companies presided over Scottish rail traffic until the Second World War, when the Government again took the reins. Following the cessation of hostilities, the election of the Labour Party to power brought Nationalisation and the formation of British Railways.

Although the railways had mostly recovered following

the First World War, the end of the second brought not only hardships for repairs, maintenance and renewals, but a much-changed world where road transport was coming to the fore. Many branch lines were ultimately lost in the 1960s as a result. The days of the steam locomotive also came to an end as part of the 'Modernisation Plan' of 1955. In Scotland, the last engine was in service during April 1967, though private industrial lines did have steam working later.

Scottish Steam 1948-1967 presents this period using nearly 250 superb colour and black-and-white images. The focus is on the various locomotives serving under BR. These ranged from old pre-Grouping locomotives still in service, such as NBR Reid and Holmes 0-6-0s, CR Pickersgill 0-4-4Ts and HR 4-4-0s, to the many LNER and LMSR designs introduced to modernise the respective motive power stocks after 1923. Gresley's J38 0-6-0s were concentrated in Scotland specifically for the coal traffic, whilst surplus Gresley K2 2-6-0s were brought north of the border to work on the West Highland line and before the war these services were given new K4 Class 2-6-0s. At the head of the principal East Coast expresses were the A1/A3 Pacifics and secondary trains had Gresley D49 Class 4-4-0s, also assisted by repurposed Robinson D11/2 'Director' Class 4-4-0s, the design of which originated on the Great Central Railway. Later, Thompson's B1 4-6-0 (many of which were constructed in Scotland by the North British Locomotive Company) was used in many areas – the GNSR territory for example – and Peppercorn's A2 Pacific took over the Edinburgh-Aberdeen traffic with success. For the LMSR, Hughes 'Crab' Class 2-6-0s were used on many freight trains on the West Coast, later assisted by Stanier's Class

5 4-6-0, which also worked passenger trains. The principal expresses were the domain of Stanier 'Coronation' Class Pacifics, as well as Stanier 'Jubilee' 4-6-0s. Local trains were often handled by Fairburn 2-6-4T locomotives which were based on the successful Fowler/Stanier predecessors.

At Nationalisation, many of the top positions in BR were filled by ex-LMSR men and this influenced locomotive policy. The Fairburn 2-6-4T was taken and developed as the BR Standard Class 4, finding employment on Glasgow suburban services, whilst the Stanier Class 5 formed the basis of BR Standard Class 5. This saw an experiment made with British Caprotti valve gear and poppet valves, with 30 of the class fitted. Both varieties saw use in Scotland. BR Standard Class 7 'Britannia' Pacifics were seen in Southern Scotland on main line expresses, with the slightly smaller Standard Class 6 Pacific mainly concentrated in the country and named after 'Clans'. Many heavier freight duties were handled by ex-War Department 'Austerity' 2-8-0s that were brought into service under BR from the many surplus engines from the war.

The locomotives featured have been pictured at many locations across Scotland. From the cities of Edinburgh and Glasgow – including their environs – to points on the main lines radiating southward, such as Burnmouth and Beattock. Several places on the Waverley route are included, in addition to the Ayrshire coast. Northward, Stirling, Alloa, Dundee, Aberdeen, Perth, etc., are featured, as is the West Highland and far north of Scotland – Thurso and Wick. The images have been taken at the lineside, stations, sheds, workshops and industrial locations. The book provides a fascinating record of the end of steam in Scotland.

Peter Tuffrey
Doncaster, January 2022

Above ABERDEEN FERRYHILL SHED – NO. 60919

On 14th May 1965, Gresley V2 no. 60919 is at Aberdeen Ferryhill shed for servicing. The engine had been a long-term resident there, but had moved to Dundee during 1964. Withdrawal from the latter occurred in September 1966. Photograph by Bill Reed.

Below ABERDEEN STATION – NO. 44703

Snowplough-equipped Stanier Class 5 no. 44703 has a southbound passenger train ready to depart from Aberdeen station on 30th March 1964. Photograph courtesy Rail Photoprints.

Above ABERDEEN STATION – NO. 44998

The 'Granite City' express from Aberdeen to Glasgow Buchanan Street stands behind Stanier Class 5 no. 44998 on 30th August 1965. Photograph by Geoff Warnes.

Below ABERDEEN DOCKS – NO. 3

To the north east of Aberdeen station, close to Waterloo goods station (ex-GNSR), was Aberdeen Gas Works. In 1919, the site was modernised and the locomotive stock was also upgraded at the time, with Andrew Barclay Sons & Co. providing 0-4-0ST no. 3. The locomotive is pictured c. 1960 with enclosed wheels and motion for safety reasons. No. 3 was later preserved. Photograph by Bill Reed.

Above **ABERDEEN KITTYBREWSTER SHED – NO. 65297**
Located to the north of Aberdeen station, Kittybrewster shed was opened by the Great North of Scotland Railway in the late 19th century. Ex-North British Railway Holmes J36 (NBR C) Class no. 65297 is pictured there around 1960. Photograph by Bill Reed.

Below **ABERDEEN STATION – NO. 44794**
The 12.00 southbound service from Aberdeen to Glasgow Buchanan Street is at the platform with no. 44794 in May 1966. The engine survived almost another year to April 1967. Photograph by Ian C. Turnbull courtesy Rail Photoprints.

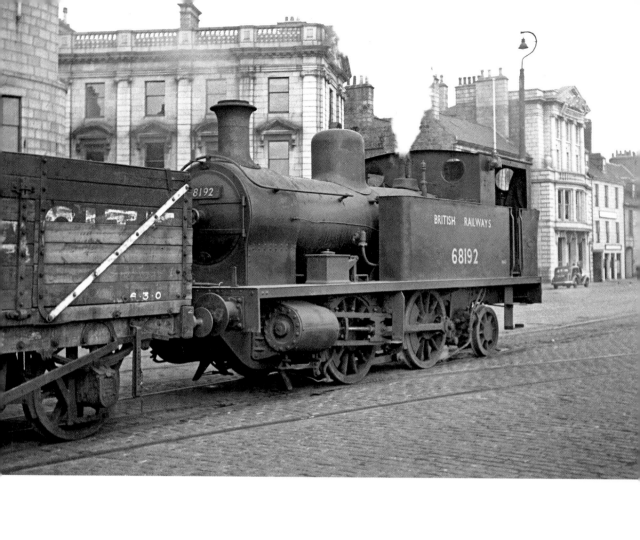

Above ALLOA – NO. 65917

At Helensfield, just east of Alloa, Gresley J38 Class 0-6-0 no. 65917 has a loaded coal train on 8th September 1966. The class was introduced in the mid-1920s for local freight and coal traffic, initially across the system, though the design was later superseded by J39 which had smaller wheels and a greater route availability. The J38s numbered just 35 and were concentrated in Scotland. No. 65917 was erected at Darlington Works in March 1926 as LNER no. 1420 and new to Dunfermline. The locomotive was allocated there through to May 1949 when transferred to Polmont. No. 65917 was there to May 1964, after which spells at Grangemouth and Thornton Junction occurred. Returning to Dunfermline in August of that year, the locomotive was condemned in November 1966. Photograph by David Christie.

Opposite above ABERDEEN DOCKS – NO. 68192

Shunting along Regent Quay, at the junction with Marischal Street, Aberdeen, is ex-GNSR Class Y, LNER Z5, 0-4-2T no. 68192. The locomotive was bought from Manning Wardle specifically for work at Aberdeen Dock and was one of two completed in 1915. Yet, these were too heavy for the dockside lines and were often restricted in fuel capacities in order to compromise with the authorities. The GNSR was obliged to purchase two more locomotives (GNSR X, LNER Z4) later in the year which were five tons lighter. The Z5s often found themselves in store during later years and could be hired by local companies for use when needed. No. 68192 is employed by British Railways here on 1st August 1950. Photograph from the Ranwell Collection courtesy Rail Photoprints.

Opposite below ABERDEEN KITTYBREWSTER SHED – NO. 62493

Stabling facilities for the Great North of Scotland Railway's locomotives were provided at Aberdeen on the west side of Kittybrewster station in the mid-1850s. This was a straight shed and later in the 19th century was replaced by a half roundhouse. The building was in use through to June 1961 when closed by British Railways. Reid D34 (NBR K) Class 4-4-0 no. 62493 *Glen Gloy* is on the turntable at the shed during the mid-1950s. The locomotive was allocated to the depot in 1953 and remained employed there to withdrawal in June 1960. Photograph courtesy Rail Photoprints.

ALLOA STATION – NO. 61029

Thompson B1 Class 4-6-0 no. 61029 *Chamois* leads a train of metal coal hopper wagons through Alloa station on 8th September 1966. Thornton Junction-allocated at the time, withdrawal occurred at the end of the year following brief tenures at Dunfermline and Dundee. Photograph by David Christie.

Above ALLOA STATION – NO. 65912
Joining the Stirling-Dunfermline line from the Devon Valley branch with a fully-loaded coal train is Gresley J38 no. 65912. Pictured on 7th September 1966, the locomotive was sent for scrap just two months later. Photograph by David Christie.

Below ALLOA STATION – NO. 90386
War Department 'Austerity' Class 2-8-0 no. 90386 is coupled to a train of coal hopper wagons at Alloa station on 8th September 1966. Photograph by David Christie.

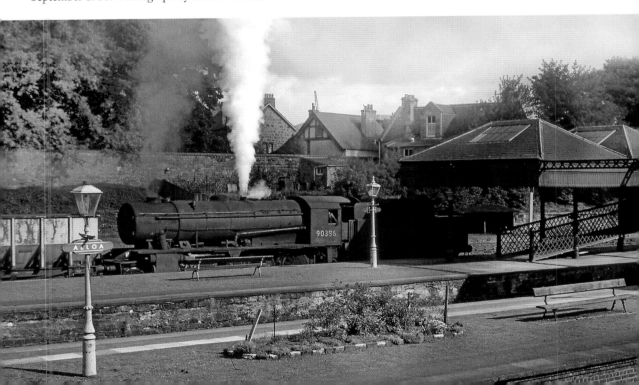

Above ARISAIG – NO. 61997

After the first Gresley K4, no. 3441, proved successful in service on the West Highland line, a further five engines were ordered and built in 1938/1939. No. 3442 was the first of these and in traffic for July 1938. At Glasgow Eastfield shed the engine's original name, *MacCailein Mór* was removed soon after and *The Great Marquess* substituted. The reason for the change is unclear and the aforementioned name later appeared on no. 3445, with a different spelling, *MacCailin Mor*. The latter, seen here as BR no. 61997, is between Mallaig and Fort William at Arisaig on 10th September 1958. The engine has a mixed freight/passenger train for Glasgow Queen Street. Photograph by David Anderson courtesy Rail Photoprints.

Opposite above ALLOA STATION – NO. 64585

In late summer 1850, the Stirling & Dunfermline Railway completed a section of the line from Oakley (west of Dunfermline) to Alloa. The station at the latter was opened as the terminus, but by the middle of the decade became a through station for Stirling and Alloa Ferry, which crossed the River Forth. During the mid-1880s, Alloa station was improved following the opening of two branches and the connection to the Caledonian Railway over the river. The original station was to the west of Erskine Street and when rebuilt was just west of there with access to the island platform gained from the roadway. Reid J37 Class 0-6-0 no. 64585 has a train of empties passing through Alloa station on 4th March 1964. The station was closed by the end of the decade, only to be resurrected in the mid-2000s east of the second site. Photograph by Sid Rickard from the J&J Collection courtesy Rail Photoprints.

Opposite below ARBROATH STATION – NO. 67493

Reid introduced the 4-4-2T wheel arrangement to the NBR in 1911 for the company's suburban and short distance passenger trains. These engines were the M Class and had saturated boilers. The L Class was a continuation of these but with a superheated boiler and 21 were constructed between 1915 and 1921. Classified C16 by the LNER, this locomotive, no. 67493 (as NBR no. 449) was amongst those and erected at the North British Locomotive Company's Atlas Works in April 1916. Pictured in the 1950s with a local service for Dundee at Arbroath station, the engine left Edinburgh for Dundee after Nationalisation and was withdrawn from Thornton Junction in April 1956. Photograph courtesy Rail-Online.

Above AYR SHED – NO. 42789
Hughes 'Crab' Class 2-6-0 no. 42789 is in the shed yard at Ayr during July 1966. Built at Crewe Works in October 1927, the engine's career was shortly to end in November 1966. Photograph by Charlie Cross from the Gordon Edgar Collection courtesy Rail Photoprints.

Below AYR SHED – NO. 42737
Another 'Crab' Class locomotive, no. 42789, is at Ayr shed, in this instance on 14th July 1965. The depot had employed the locomotive from January 1961 and did so to withdrawal in November 1966, just before Ayr closed to steam. Photograph by Bill Wright.

Above AYR SHED – NO. 42803

Though an open smokebox door on a locomotive in a shed yard often denoted being out of service, even at this late date, 24th April 1966, 'Crab' Class no. 42803 was in steam and working from Ayr. The engine went on to have a brief spell at Motherwell before condemned in late November 1966. Photograph by Bill Wright.

Below AYR SHED – NO. 44724 AND NO. 45177

A pair of Stanier Class 5 4-6-0s stand in the yard at Ayr on 24th April 1966. No. 44724 was a late example, being constructed at Crewe during April 1949, whilst no. 45177 was an early class member and built by Armstrong Whitworth & Co. in September 1935. The latter was sent for scrap in July and no. 44724 left traffic at the end of the year. Photograph by Bill Wright.

Above BALLACHULISH STATION – NO. 55263

Ballachulish station was opened on 20th August 1903 by the Callander & Oban Railway and located on Loch Leven's south shore at Glencoe in the Highlands. The station was the terminus of the branch from Connel Ferry on the line to Oban and was renamed soon after opening to Ballachulish & Glencoe, later becoming Ballachulish (Glencoe) for Kinlochleven which remained in use to closure in March 1966. No. 55263 was one of ten 2P 0-4-4T locomotives built by Nasmyth Wilson in 1925 for the London Midland & Scottish Railway and based on William Pickersgill's 431 Class constructed before Grouping. No. 55263 was in traffic from May 1925 to October 1961. The engine has a local service for Connel Ferry in 1957. Photograph from the John Day Collection courtesy Rail Photoprints.

Opposite above AYR STATION – NO. 42196 AND 40602

Fairburn 4P Class 2-6-4T no. 42196 is light engine at the platform, whilst Fowler 2P Class 4-4-0 no. 40602 arrives at Ayr station with a short local passenger train from Kilmarnock on 22nd June 1961. The latter engine was shortly to be withdrawn from service in October, following just over a year's employment at Hurlford shed (east of Kilmarnock). No. 42196 had been at Ayr for nearly ten years at this point, though had been new to Glasgow Corkerhill in February 1948. In September 1962 the locomotive moved on to Hurlford, but soon after transferred to Dumfries. A year later, the engine crossed into England for a role at Leeds Neville Hill and was at Bradford Low Moor when condemned during May 1967. Photograph by Sid Rickard from the J&J Collection courtesy Rail Photoprints.

Opposite below BACK O' LOCH HALT – NO. 64611

Following the foundation of the Edinburgh & Glasgow Railway, a gradual northward expansion from Lenzie through the Campsie Fells to the Stirling-Balloch route was made, becoming a branch that eventually reached Aberfoyle. Shortly after Grouping, the LNER opened a new halt on the line between Lenzie and Kirkintilloch – Back o' Loch – to increase the area served and ward off the road transport threat. Here, on 27th January 1962, Reid J37 Class 0-6-0 no. 64611 has a loaded coal train from Kilsyth. The branch from Lenzie also connected with the mineral line between Larbert and Maryhill. Back o' Loch halt closed in 1964 and the line was lifted. Photograph by Sid Rickard from the J&J Collection courtesy Rail Photoprints.

Above BALLACHULISH FERRY STATION
A small station was built on the Ballachulish branch to serve the ferry across Loch Leven, opening in August 1903. This later closed for a time during the First World War and again in 1953. Ballachulish Ferry station, pictured on 28th September 1961, was in use to 1966. Photograph by B.W.L. Brooksbank.

Opposite above BALLATER STATION
Before the Royal Family made a connection with Balmoral, west of Ballater, there were plans to lay a line from Aberdeen into the area during the 'Railway Mania' of the mid-1840s. When this 'bubble' collapsed, the project was to follow suit until Prince Albert took the Balmoral property in the late 1840s. The route went on to be built in stages between 1853 and 1866, with three companies completing these. The first left the main line at Ferryhill Junction (just north of the engine shed) and reached Banchory under the Deeside Railway. The next part on to Aboyne was constructed by the Deeside Extension Railway in 1859 and the Aboyne & Braemar Railway completed the 43-mile route in 1866. This was later taken over by the Great North of Scotland Railway. A desolate scene has been captured at Ballater station on 3rd October 1961. Operations continued to 1966 when all services were withdrawn and the line lifted. The station survived, however, and later became a tourist attraction. A fire destroyed the building in 2015, though an extensive restoration has returned the station to former glories. Photograph by B.W.L. Brooksbank.

Opposite below BANCHORY STATION
On 2nd October 1961, the station at Banchory has been captured in a similar state of idleness to Ballater station. Banchory also closed with the line in 1966 and was later demolished. Photograph by B.W.L. Brooksbank.

Above BANFF BRIDGE STATION
A view of Banff Bridge station on the branch from Inveramsay to Macduff, 2nd October 1961. Goods services had been withdrawn recently, whilst passenger trains failed to stop there from October 1951; the building still stands today. Photograph by B.W.L. Brooksbank.

Below BALLINLUIG – NO. 54499
A local service is heading for Perth on 5th July 1957 and pictured to the north at Ballinluig. The train is led by Pickersgill 72 Class 4-4-0 no. 54499. Photograph by David Anderson courtesy Rail Photoprints.

Above BATHGATE – NO. 64569

From January 1962 to November 1964, Reid J37 Class no. 64569 was employed at Bathgate (between Edinburgh and Glasgow). The engine is pictured there on 13th May 1963. Photograph by Sid Rickard from the J&J Collection courtesy Rail Photoprints.

Below BARGEDDIE – NO. 62680

At Grouping, a motive power shortage in the North British area saw Gresley turn to J.G. Robinson's 11F 4-4-0 for use there. Classified D11/2, a total of 24 were erected, with no. 62680 *Lucy Ashton* completed in October 1924. The locomotive is at Bargeddie for scrap on 5th October 1961. Photograph by B.W.L. Brooksbank.

Above BATHGATE SHED – NO. 64614

Reid J37 no. 64614 is at Bathgate shed on 29th May 1964. A recent arrival in February, the engine survived to the end of the year after 44 years in traffic. Photograph courtesy Rail Photoprints.

Below BATHGATE SHED – NO. 65282

A long-term servant at Bathgate depot was no. 65282. The engine is in the yard on 15th July 1965, six months before sent for scrap. Photograph by Bill Wright.

Above BATHGATE – NO. 69156
In the goods yard at Bathgate, Reid N15 Class 0-6-2T no. 69156 is shunting coal wagons on 27th September 1957. Photograph by B.W.L. Brooksbank.

Below BATHGATE SHED
A trio of Reid J36 0-6-0s are in the yard at Bathgate shed on 19th September 1962. On the left is no. 65341, a long-term resident, no. 65277 is middle and recently returned to Bathgate from Keith. No. 65261 is right and another servant from at least Nationalisation. All were condemned at Bathgate in mid-1963. Photograph by B.W.L. Brooksbank.

Above BEATTOCK NO. 42694

The highest point on the West Coast Main Line was Beattock Summit, 52 miles from Glasgow. Steep gradients were present on the 10-mile climb to 1,016 ft above sea level. Fairburn 4P no. 42694 is engaged as assistant for Class 5 no. 45176, which has a mineral train, on 31st May 1966. Photograph by Hugh Ballantyne courtesy Rail Photoprints.

Opposite above BEATTOCK – NO. 73098

Glasgow Polmadie-allocated BR Standard Class 5 4-6-0 no. 73098 gets away from Beattock station after stopping for assistance on 25th July 1964. This service was provided by Standard Class 4 4-6-0 no. 76090. Photograph courtesy Rail Photoprints.

Opposite below BEATTOCK STATION – NO. 44955

An express parcels train passes through Beattock station on 6th October 1961. Stanier Class 5 no. 44955 is at the head of the train and was working from Carstairs at the time. Photograph by B.W.L. Brooksbank.

Opposite above BISHOPBRIGGS – NO. 64523

On the Edinburgh to Glasgow line at Bishopbriggs, Reid J35 Class 0-6-0 no. 64523 has a westbound freight. Pictured on 15th October 1960, the locomotive was Parkhead-allocated at the time and had been there a year following a transfer from Edinburgh St Margaret's. No. 64523 was condemned just a short time later in February 1961. Photograph by Sid Rickard from the J&J Collection courtesy Rail Photoprints.

Opposite below BISHOPBRIGGS – NO. 43138

H.G. Ivatt designed the 4MT 2-6-0 after the Second World War for both passenger and freight duties. One of the main considerations of the design was ease of maintenance, resulting in the high, if ungainly, running plate to allow complete access to oiling points. No. 43138 appeared from Doncaster Works in July 1951 and was new to Glasgow Eastfield. When photographed on 6th May 1961 at Bishopbriggs with eastbound empty mineral wagons, the engine was allocated to Parkhead, though was soon to transfer to England. Photograph by Sid Rickard from the J&J Collection courtesy Rail Photoprints.

Below BLAIR ATHOLL STATION

The Inverness & Perth Junction Railway named Blair Atholl station 'Blair Athole' when opened on 9th September 1863. The station was on the line between Forres and Dunkeld and this was completed in three sections; Blair Atholl was on the final part. This image was captured there on 13th September 1962, with BR Type 2 diesel no. D5120 disappearing northbound with a freight train. The station continues to serve passengers. Photograph by B.W.L. Brooksbank.

Above BOGSIDE – NO. 65288
Face to face at Bogside (east of Alloa) on 8th September 1966 is Holmes J36 Class 0-6-0 no. 65288 and an unidentified WD 'Austerity' 2-8-0. Photograph by David Christie.

Below BOGSIDE – NO. 65917
Another engine working through Bogside is Gresley J38 no. 65917. Photograph by David Christie.

Above BLACKFORD HILL – NO. 61911

Gresley K3 2-6-0 no. 61911 travels along the Edinburgh avoiding line at Blackford Hill with a freight train on 19th June 1957. Photograph by David Anderson courtesy Rail Photoprints.

Below BRIDGE OF DUN – NO. 60034

The 13.30 train from Aberdeen to Glasgow has stopped at Bridge of Dun during July 1965. Gresley A4 Pacific no. 60034 *Lord Faringdon* heads the service. Photograph by Brian Robbins courtesy Rail Photoprints.

Above BRIDGE OF ALLAN – NO. 60034

The introduction of diesel locomotives at the southern end of the East Coast Main Line occurred in the early 1960s and by 1963 steam was banned south of Peterborough. This edict displaced a number of still capable Pacifics, mainly Gresley engines which had been revitalised recently with the fitting of double chimneys. Whilst some were scrapped, a number of A4s were employed in the Scottish Region on the Glasgow Buchanan Street to Aberdeen expresses. Some of these were tightly timed at three hours, but the A4s were more than equal to the challenge, despite being 30 years old. No. 60034 *Lord Faringdon* transferred northward in October 1963, first reaching Edinburgh St Margaret's, then moving on to Aberdeen in May 1964. The engine served on the route for just over two years and is pictured a year before withdrawal on 23rd August 1965 at Bridge of Allan (north of Stirling) with an express. Photograph by David Christie.

Opposite above BURNMOUTH – NO. 64925

On 3rd July 1961, Gresley J39 0-6-0 no. 64925 is at Burnmouth station with a local service for Eyemouth. Opened in the late 1840s by the North British Railway, Burnmouth station was the junction for the Eyemouth branch from 13th April 1891. The line was built by the Eyemouth Railway and later taken over by the NBR at the turn of the century. Both Burnmouth and the branch had just over six months left in operation as closure occurred on 5th February 1962. No. 64925 lasted to the end of that year and was one of the final J39s in traffic. Photograph by Bill Reed.

Opposite below CADDER – NO. 64610

Just west of Lenzie, the NBR established a goods yard at Cadder around the turn of the century. Reid J37 Class 0-6-0 no. 64610 is passing there with an eastbound rake of empty mineral wagons on 12th May 1962. Built by the NBLC in January 1920, the locomotive was in service to February 1966 when condemned at Dunfermline. Photograph by Sid Rickard from the J&J Collection courtesy Rail Photoprints.

Opposite above CALLANDER – NO. 45158
Stanier Class 5 no. 45158 *Glasgow Yeomanry* is at Callander station with a local train between Oban and Glasgow on 3rd April 1961. The locomotive was amongst four named in the mid-1930s after Scottish army regiments and received *Glasgow Yeomanry* in May 1936. As a result, no. 45158 was a long-term St Rollox shed resident and did not move until early 1964. The engine has also received an extra adornment in the form of a small snow plough. Photograph by Sid Rickard from the J&J Collection courtesy Rail Photoprints.

Opposite below CARSTAIRS SHED – NO. 54461
Pickersgill 72 Class 4-4-0 no. 54461 spent two periods in store at Carstairs shed, with the first lasting several months between late 1951 and early 1952, then the second covered much of the second half of 1953. The locomotive is pictured shortly into the second spell on 21st June 1953. Photograph by B.W.L. Brooksbank.

Below CARSTAIRS – NO. 54461
Located to the south west of Glasgow, Carstairs was an important point on the Caledonian Railway Main Line in the area, as several routes converged. One was a line from Midcalder Junction on the Edinburgh-Glasgow route serving collieries in the area, whilst a branch also headed eastward to Dolphinton, meeting the NBR, yet no through service was offered. Westward, the lines reached Lanark and Muirkirk where the Glasgow & South Western Railway to Ayr, Kilmarnock, etc., was met. At Carstairs on 17th September 1950 is Pickersgill 72 Class 4-4-0 no. 54461, which has an engineer's train. The engine was the first of the type built at St Rollox Works in February 1916. For much of the BR period, no. 54461 was engaged at Carstairs shed. Photograph by David Anderson courtesy Rail Photoprints.

Above CLACKMANNAN – NO. 65912
East of Alloa, Gresley J38 no. 65912 has a train of coal wagons at Clackmannan on 8th September 1966. Just two months remained for the locomotive. Photograph by David Christie.

Below CLACKMANNAN – NO. 65934
Another J38 at Clackmannan, on the same day as above, is no. 65934. Built at Darlington Works in May 1926, the engine was in service to the end of 1966. No. 65934 has a ballast train here. Photograph by David Christie.

Above COATBRIDGE – NO. 46118

A sad scene captured in the scrapyard of J.N. Connell Ltd, Coatbridge, during November 1964. Fowler 'Royal Scot' no. 46118 *Royal Welch Fusilier* is in the midst of dismantling, but an interesting view of the firebox stays is revealed. Photograph by David Anderson courtesy Rail Photoprints.

Below COVE BAY – NO. 60094

Gresley A3 no. 60094 *Colorado* has the 17.15 Aberdeen to Glasgow service at Cove Bay on 26th April 1963. Photograph from the Dave Cobbe Collection courtesy Rail Photoprints.

Above CRAIGELLACHIE – NO. 62270 AND NO. 62269
Two Pickersgill D40 (GNSR V) Class 4-4-0s, no. 62270 and no. 62269, are near Craigellachie with a freight train bound for Keith on 29th March 1952. Photograph by W.J. Verden Anderson from Rail Archive Stephenson courtesy Rail-Online.

Opposite COWLAIRS – NO. 60537
The Edinburgh & Glasgow Railway was authorised in 1838. Beginning at Edinburgh Haymarket, the line took a northern course – where the land was favourable – and paralleled the Union Canal, which, from 1822, connected Edinburgh with the Forth & Clyde. Unfortunately, the canal companies were directly affronted by this and successfully thwarted the E&GR from passing over the Forth & Clyde at Port Dundas, Glasgow. As a result, the railway was forced underneath the waterway by means of a long, steep tunnel to the station, which faced on to George Street. From the opening on 21st February 1842 until the early 20th century, the Cowlairs bank (with gradients around 1 in 41) was operated by a rope haulage system. Soon, the limitations of using ropes to drag the trains up Cowlairs incline became very apparent through frequent breakages and high cost of replacing the equipment. Two powerful locomotives to escort the trains out of the station were built instead and construction of the pair was carried out at Cowlairs Works, being the first from the shops. 0-6-0T *Hercules* was built in January 1844 with 4 ft 3½ in. diameter wheels and 15½ in. diameter cylinders, and the second - named *Sampson* - followed later in the year, being slightly modified with larger cylinders. Both locomotives performed well and reduced the cost of working the trains out to Cowlairs, but were too powerful for the time as the rails were fragile and kept breaking, leading to the reinstatement of the rope haulage system in 1847. This lasted to the early 20th century though assistance still had to be provided on occasion. One instance has been captured here on 25th May 1956, as Peppercorn A2 Class Pacific no. 60537 *Bachelors Button* leaves Queen Street station with the 11.00 train and has Reid N15 Class 0-6-2T no. 69181 at the rear. Photograph courtesy Rail-Online.

CRAIGENTINNY – NO. 61987

A local service is at Craigentinny, east of Edinburgh, behind Gresley K3 Class 2-6-0 no. 61987 in the 1950s.
Photograph courtesy Rail-Online.

Above COWLAIRS WORKS – NO. 61349
Thompson B1 no. 61349 has entered Cowlairs Works for refurbishments to be carried out in July 1965. This kept the engine employed until August 1966. Photograph by Brian Robbins courtesy Rail Photoprints.

Below CRAIGELLACHIE – NO. 62264
Pickersgill D40 Class 4-4-0 no. 62264 has reached Craigellachie with a local train from Boat of Garten on 4th July 1951. A displaced Great Eastern Railway Holden B12 Class 4-6-0, no. 61560, is at the adjacent platform with the 17.46 service between Keith and Elgin. Photograph courtesy Rail-Online.

Opposite above DALMENY – NO. 61789

Gresley K2 Class 2-6-0 no. 61789 has just crossed the Forth Bridge and reached Dalmeny station with a Dunfermline to Glasgow train on 13th August 1955. The Edinburgh & Glasgow Railway opened the first station at Dalmeny on 1st March 1866, but this was later replaced at the opening of the Forth Bridge in 1890. No. 61789 was built at Kitson & Co. for the Great Northern Railway in August 1921. When the class was superseded by new engines on the ECML, a number were dispatched to work on the West Highland Line and no. 61789 arrived at Glasgow Eastfield in April 1925. Subsequently, several were named after nearby Lochs in recognition of their service there, and the engine received *Loch Laidon* in June 1934. Later in the decade the locomotive was based at Fort William and was there throughout the 1940s, returning to Glasgow in the early 1950s. Withdrawal from there occurred in September 1959. Photograph by David Anderson courtesy Rail Photoprints.

Opposite below DALMENY – NO. 60528

A short distance on from Dalmeny station, Peppercorn A2 Pacific no. 60528 *Tudor Minstrel* has an Aberdeen to Edinburgh express on 23rd May 1959. Photograph by David Anderson courtesy Rail Photoprints.

Below CROY – NO. 90472

When the war machine scaled up in the early 1940s, the War Department needed large numbers of locomotives to move men and materials in the conflict theatres around the world. The Stanier 8F 2-8-0 design was taken and simplified to create the 'Austerity' Class of which nearly 1,000 were erected. Of these, 733 were taken into stock by British Railways. No. 90472 was constructed by Vulcan Foundry in June 1944 and in late 1945 was employed by the London & North Eastern Railway at Thornton Junction. The locomotive is one of the very few 'Austerity' Class to have just one allocation and was at the depot through to withdrawal in December 1963. No. 90472 is at Croy (west of Falkirk) with a train of coal wagons in August 1963. Photograph by Geoff Warnes.

Above DINGWALL SHED – NO. 54471
The line northward from Inverness was completed in the early 1860s, though locomotive servicing facilities at Dingwall were not present until 1870 when a two-track timber structure was erected at the south end of the station. Pictured outside the shed building on 26th September 1957 is Pickersgill 113 Class 4-4-0 no. 54471. The locomotive was allocated to Forres at this time and was there until condemned during October 1959 following nearly 44 years in service. Photograph by B.W.L. Brooksbank.

Opposite above DINGWALL – NO. 14401
Peter Drummond 'Ben' Class 4-4-0 no. 14401 *Ben Vrackie* is at Dingwall station on 25th August 1948. The engine was one of twenty built for the Highland Railway between 1898 and 1906 and a further six similar engines with larger boilers were constructed in 1908/1909. No. 14401 was built at Dübs & Co. in February 1899 as HR no. 5 and was in traffic to October 1948. In front of the locomotive is a Tredegar Colliery (South Wales) seven-plank coal wagon which had been taken into common stock in the Second World War. Photograph by B.W.L. Brooksbank.

Opposite below DINGWALL – NO. 55199
The Caledonian Railway produced a number of 0-4-4T locomotives between 1884 and Grouping. The 439 Class appeared in 1895 and numbered 92 examples by 1925. No. 55199 was built at St Rollox Works in December 1909 as no. 456, later receiving LMSR number 15199. The locomotive is pictured at Dingwall shed on 26th September 1957, being prepared for the next duty. No. 55199 was a long-term resident at Inverness shed. Withdrawal occurred in July 1961. Photograph by B.W.L. Brooksbank.

Above DUMFRIES STATION – NO. 40614

A northbound train from Dumfries station to Kilmarnock is at the platform and ready to depart behind no. 40614 in 1959. Dating from 1848, the station connected to Glasgow from Kilmarnock, whilst also having two junctions with the Caledonian main line at Lockerbie and Gretna. Furthermore, there were branches to Moniaive and Kirkcudbright, with the latter providing access to Stranraer. No. 40614 was allocated to Dumfries throughout the BR period and was withdrawn in October 1961. Photograph from the Dave Cobbe Collection courtesy Rail Photoprints.

Opposite above DRUMOCHTER – NO. 44980

The line from Perth to Inverness was only able to thread a path through the Grampian Mountains at the Pass of Drumochter (south of Dalwhinnie). Northbound trains had a climb of around 18 miles from Blair Atholl to the summit (1,484 ft), with the gradient mainly 1 in 70. Trains travelling southward had a similar obstacle to overcome, though not quite as difficult at 1 in 100 dropping to 1 in 80 for a stretch. Stanier Class 5 no. 44980 has almost completed the northward climb here on 26th September 1957 with a train primarily consisting of loaded coal wagons. The route between Perth and Inverness was mainly single track, but double line was present on the climb to Drumochter and ten miles to Inverness. Photograph by B.W.L. Brooksbank.

Opposite below DINGWALL STATION – NO. 54463

The Inverness & Ross-shire Railway reached Dingwall as part of the first stage of the project to reach Invergordon in June 1862. The second part was ready for traffic in March 1863, yet by this time the company had been absorbed into the Inverness & Aberdeen Junction Railway. The original station was later replaced by a new structure in the early 1880s and at this point the Highland Railway was in charge of operations in the area. Pickersgill 113 Class 4-4-0 no. 54463 is at Dingwall station with an Inverness-bound train on 9th September 1958. Photograph by David Anderson courtesy Rail Photoprints.

DUMFRIES STATION – NO. 80117
An excursion organised by the Gainsborough Model Railway Society ran from Lincoln to Dumfries on 15th May 1965. No. 4472 *Flying Scotsman* was the engine, seen taking water here in front of BR Standard Class 4 2-6-4T no. 80117. Photograph by Geoff Warnes.

Above DUMFRIES – NO. 42907
Hughes 'Crab' Class 2-6-0 no. 42907 departs from Dumfries with a mixed freight train destined for Kilmarnock in September 1959. Photograph from the Dave Cobbe Collection courtesy Rail Photoprints.

Below DUMFRIES – NO. 76073
Also pictured at Dumfries station on 15th May 1965 are two light engines, BR Standard Class 4 2-6-0 no. 76073 and Stanier Class 5 no. 45463. Photograph by Geoff Warnes.

DUNDEE – NO. 64620
Reid J37 Class no. 64620 has a train of tank wagons at Dundee in July 1966. Many are branded 'Briggs, Dundee' with the company operating an oil refinery. Photograph by Brian Robbins courtesy Rail Photoprints.

Above DUNBLANE – NO. 60009
North of Stirling at Dunblane, Gresley A4 no. 60009 *Union of South Africa* has the 'Bon Accord' service between Aberdeen and Glasgow on 23rd August 1965. Photograph by David Christie.

Below DUNBLANE – NO. 73148
A southbound train of empty coaching stock is at Dunblane on 26th August 1965 with tender-first BR Standard Class 5 no. 73148. The engine was amongst the class members fitted with Caprotti valve gear. Photograph by David Christie.

Above DUNDEE TAY BRIDGE STATION – NO. 80124

As part of British Railway's Standard Classes, a tank engine for commuter traffic was included in the building programme to meet deficiencies in the stock of the Southern and Scottish Regions. The Standard Class 4 2-6-4T was based on the successful Fowler/Stanier/Fairburn version built in numbers for the London Midland & Scottish Railway and eventually totalled 155 examples. No. 80124 was one of one hundred and thirty erected at Brighton Works and the locomotive arrived new at Dundee Tay Bridge shed during September 1955. The engine is pictured departing from Dundee station with a local service on 28th March 1964. At the start of 1966, no. 80124 moved south to Edinburgh St Margaret's and was condemned there in December 1966. Photograph by Neville Simms from the Ranwell Collection courtesy Rail Photoprints.

Opposite above DUNDEE ESPLANADE STATION – NO. 61102

Opened with the second bridge in 1889, Dundee Esplanade station was located just off the structure on the north bank of the River Tay. The facility was in use to 1917, then closed for two years and again opened, this lasting to just after the start of the Second World War. Reopening for a third time failed to occur. Thompson B1 Class no. 61102 has a train of coal wagons passing the station buildings on 21st May 1965. The locomotive was new to Dundee Tay Bridge shed in December 1946 and remained employed there until condemned in April 1967. Photograph courtesy Rail-Online.

Opposite below DUNDEE TAY BRIDGE STATION – NO. 60528 AND NO. 60532

Edward Thompson's mixed traffic 6 ft 2 in. A2/3 Pacifics suffered from having the bogie positioned so far forward, creating stresses at the front end that caused fractures and leakages of the exhaust steam passages. His successor A.H. Peppercorn remedied this defect on his own A2 Pacific design and 15 were built, with the first entering traffic just before Nationalisation and bearing his name. Initially based in England, many of the class were soon dispatched to Scotland to work between Edinburgh and Aberdeen, with engines changed at Dundee. A pair of A2s is in the yard at Tay Bridge shed on 30th August 1965. With tender end prominent is no. 60528 *Tudor Minstrel*, whilst stood behind is no. 60532 *Blue Peter*. The latter became the only Peppercorn Pacific to be preserved. Photograph by B.W.L. Brooksbank.

DUNDEE TAY BRIDGE SHED – NO. 64620

Reid J37 Class no. 64620 is outside the six-road depot at Dundee Tay Bridge in the 1960s. Photograph by Bill Reed.

Above DUNDEE TAY BRIDGE SHED – NO. 64619

Another Reid J37 Class 0-6-0, no. 64619, is at Dundee Tay Bridge shed in the 1960s. Though built for express freight duties under the NBR, after Nationalisation local duties usually prevailed. Dundee always had several on hand. Photograph by Bill Reed.

Below DUNDEE – NO. 62485

The CR had a shed at Dundee (just to the west of Tay Bridge depot) which BR closed in the late 1950s. For a time, this area was used to store locomotives, which is the case for Reid D34 'Glen' Class 4-4-0 no. 62485 *Glen Murran* here. Photograph by Bill Reed.

Above DUNFERMLINE LOWER STATION – NO. 64599

After the Edinburgh & Glasgow Railway consolidated their position with that important line, expansion occurred over the Firth of Forth and tracks were laid between Stirling, Alloa and Dunfermline. The station opened on this route in December 1849. Though a bridge over the Firth was planned, that over the Tay was prioritised and initial enthusiasm from the NBR for a connection between Dunfermline and North Queensferry – the site of the crossing – dissipated leading to an independent project. This ran into financial difficulties and was taken over by the NBR, being completed in the mid-1870s, with a second station at Dunfermline opened as Dunfermline Comely Park, south of the original station there. When the Forth Bridge was completed in 1890, a new station replaced Comely Park and both were renamed at the time Dunfermline Lower and Dunfermline Upper respectively. Reid J37 Class no. 64599 is taking water at the aforementioned on 1st September 1965. Three years later, Upper station closed and Lower became Dunfermline, but has since become Dunfermline Town. Photograph by John Arnott-Brown courtesy A1 Steam Trust.

Opposite above DUNFERMLINE – NO. 65903

From the introduction of the J38 Class, a number were based at Dunfermline. There, employment was found on goods and coal trains northward to Dundee and Perth, southward to Edinburgh and westward to Glasgow. Whilst other sheds lost their J38s when withdrawals began, Dunfermline continued to have several for similar duties. No. 65903 was one of these and resided there from February 1961 to November 1966 when withdrawn; the last J38 went to the scrapyard in April 1967. The locomotive is pictured at Dunfermline in July 1966. Photograph by Paul Claxton courtesy Rail Photoprints.

Opposite below EDINBURGH WAVERLEY STATION – NO. 80122

On 30th July 1963, BR Standard Class 4 2-6-4T no. 80122 arrives at Edinburgh Waverley station with a train of empty coaching stock. The locomotive was new to Aberdeen Kittybrewster in August 1955, though by the end of the year had been sent north to Keith. During July 1961, the next move to Edinburgh Dalry Road occurred and after a year transferred across the city to St Margaret's depot. The final allocation was to Greenock in December 1965 and withdrawal took place in the following December. Class mate and shed mate no. 80022 is also visible. Photograph by Revd J. David Benson courtesy A1 Steam Trust.

Above EDINBURGH – NO. 9148

East of Edinburgh Waverley station in the Craigentinny/Portobello area, Reid N15 Class 0-6-2T no. 9148 has a westbound freight train on 16th August 1948. The engine was St Margaret's-allocated and went on to be condemned there in June 1958. Photograph by B.W.L. Brooksbank.

Below EDINBURGH – NO. 2673

Robinson D11/2 Class 4-4-0 no. 2673 *Evan Dhu* has an Edinburgh to Glasgow local train west of Edinburgh Haymarket (the shed's coaler is in the background) on 18th August 1948. Renumbered from 6380 in September 1946, the BR number was applied from the end of 1948. The engine was Eastfield-allocated through to withdrawal in July 1959. Photograph by B.W.L. Brooksbank.

Above EDINBURGH DALRY ROAD – NO. 42273

The Caledonian Railway reached Edinburgh in early 1848 with a line from Carstairs. Expansion followed to rival the North British Railway and the CR later dominated the west side to Granton and made inroads to Leith, both being important dock areas. A branch to these two places left the line from Carstairs at Dalry Road and this was the site for a station, as well as a locomotive shed. The latter is visible here to the left, whilst the tail end of the platform is visible to the right of the brake van. Several sheds existed on the site, with the first erected in 1848 and succeeded by a four-road structure in 1895, though this was later rebuilt. The branch to Leith and Granton was open from 1861, yet a station at Dalry Road was not provided until 1900 and this served passengers until 1962. Fairburn 4P Class 2-6-4T no. 42273 is featured on an empty stock train from Princes Street station to Slateford carriage sidings on 19th September 1962. The locomotive was built at Derby Works in May 1947 and had a service life of 19 years, being withdrawn in September 1966. By this time the ex-CR line from Carstairs to Princes Street had been closed and trains diverted to Waverley. Photograph by B.W.L. Brooksbank.

Above EDINBURGH DALRY ROAD SHED

A crowded yard has been captured at Edinburgh Dalry Road shed in August 1962. Present in the background is Fairburn 4P Class 2-6-4T no. 42273, BR Standard Class 4 2-6-0 no. 76105, whilst in the foreground are Pickersgill 300 Class 0-6-0 no. 57654, Stanier Class 5 no. 45036, Lambie 19 Class 0-4-4T no. 55124 and Stanier Class 5 no. 45469. Photograph by D.J. Dippie.

Below EDINBURGH DALRY ROAD SHED – NO. 57565

Circa 1960, one of the first 812 Class 0-6-0s, no. 57565 is at Dalry Road depot. Photograph by Bill Reed.

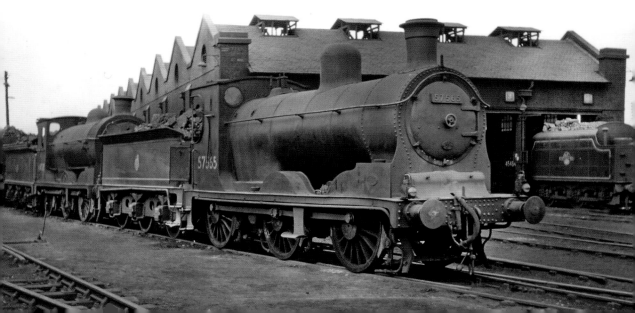

Above EDINBURGH DALRY ROAD SHED – NO. 42273
Fairburn 4P Class 2-6-4T no. 42273 was new to Dalry Road and later had a short spell at St Margaret's before condemned. The engine is next to the aforementioned shed building in August 1962; note the snowplough to the left and the diesel shunter, right. Photograph by D.J. Dippie.

Below EDINBURGH DALRY ROAD SHED – NO. 57645
The final McIntosh 652 Class 0-6-0, no. 57645, is pictured at Dalry Road shed in the 1960s. Erected in June 1909, the locomotive was in service to November 1962. Photograph by Bill Reed.

EDINBURGH HAYMARKET SHED – NO. 62709

Gresley D49 no. 62709 *Berwickshire* is in the yard at Edinburgh Haymarket shed in the late 1950s. Photograph by Bill Reed.

Above EDINBURGH HAYMARKET SHED – NO. 62685

Robinson D11/2 Class no. 62685 *Malcolm Graeme* is outside Edinburgh Haymarket shed around 1960. During the late 1950s, the class was in and out of storage, only being used at peak periods. Photograph by Bill Reed.

Below EDINBURGH HAYMARKET SHED – NO. 62719

D49 no. 62719 *Peebles-Shire* was at Edinburgh Haymarket shed from March 1943 to November 1959, then briefly at Hawick before condemned in early 1960. Photograph by Bill Reed.

EDINBURGH HAYMARKET JUNCTION – NO. 78048

An engineer's train passes under the ex-CR line to Granton and Leith while running on the Edinburgh–Glasgow line at Haymarket Junction, Edinburgh, during 1957. The engine is BR Standard Class 2 2-6-0 no. 78048. Photograph by David Anderson courtesy Rail Photoprints.

EDINBURGH HAYMARKET – NO. 60041

An Aberdeen to Edinburgh express is near Haymarket shed (coaler in the distance) behind Gresley A3 no. 60041 *Salmon Trout* on 29th September 1957. Photograph by David Anderson courtesy Rail Photoprints.

Above EDINBURGH PORTOBELLO STATION – NO. 61869
Heaton-allocated Gresley K3 no. 61869 has a local service at Portobello, east of Edinburgh, in the late 1950s. The engine was at the depot between October 1956 and January 1960. Photograph courtesy Rail-Online.

Below EDINBURGH WAVERLEY STATION – NO. 61197 AND NO. 67620
On 6th May 1957, two engines wait to depart Waverley station. Thompson B1 no. 61197 has a local train for Dundee, whilst Gresley V3 2-6-2T no. 67620 has a rake of empty stock. Photograph by Hugh Ballantyne courtesy Rail Photoprints.

Above EDINBURGH ST MARGARET'S SHED – NO. 60530

Peppercorn A2 Pacific no. 60530 *Sayajirao* waits to leave St Margaret's shed on 22nd August 1962. The locomotive was resident there between October 1961 and September 1963. Photograph courtesy Rail-Online.

Below EDINBURGH ST MARGARET'S SHED – NO. 68097

The NBR introduced 35 0-4-0ST locomotives between 1882 and 1899 to work at docks and local goods yards. A number were at St Margaret's for Leith and Granton docks, with two at St Margaret's depot resting here on 9th August 1956, no. 68097 and 68095. Photograph by Neville Simms from the Ranwell Collection courtesy Rail Photoprints.

Above EDINBURGH WAVERLEY STATION – NO. 2494

Between duties at Waverley station on 14th August 1948 is Reid 'Glen' Class 4-4-0 no. 2494 *Glen Gour*. The BR number was applied a month later, whilst the LNER number was an early switch in January 1946. Photograph by B.W.L. Brooksbank.

Below EDINBURGH WAVERLEY STATION – NO. 45727

A Perth train is at Waverley station behind Stanier 'Jubilee' no. 45727 *Inflexible* on 1st June 1957. Note the Royal Mail coach on the left. Photograph from the Gordon Edgar Collection courtesy Rail Photoprints.

Above EDINBURGH WAVERLEY STATION – NO. 62677

Robinson D11/2 no. 62677 *Edie Ochiltree* has the large style cab side number and smaller 'British Railways' lettering here on 13th August 1948. The engine is just leaving Waverley station under the Mound with a local train. Photograph by B.W.L. Brooksbank.

Below EDINBURGH PRINCES STREET GARDENS – NO. 4592

Mid-August 1948 saw a biblical deluge in the Border area seriously disrupt rail traffic. Reid J37 no. 4592 has been affected on 16th August, as freight was usually barred from passing through Waverley during the day and took the avoiding line. Photograph by B.W.L. Brooksbank.

Above ELGIN EAST STATION – NO. 62267

Pickersgill D40 (GNSR V) Class no. 62267 is at Elgin station with a local service to Lossiemouth on 26th July 1949. The BR number was applied from October 1948. Photograph courtesy Rail-Online.

Below ELGIN EAST STATION – NO. 78053

With the D40s withdrawn in the 1950s, replacements in the form of BR Standard Class 2 2-6-0s were provided. Class member no. 78053 has a train to Lossiemouth at Elgin East in the late 1950s. Photograph courtesy Rail-Online.

Above ELGIN WEST STATION – NO. 54471

Pickersgill 113 Class 4-4-0 no. 54471 has a Forres to Keith passenger train at Elgin West station on 26th August 1948. Photograph by B.W.L. Brooksbank.

Below FALKIRK GRAHAMSTON STATION – NO. 44975

Stanier Class 5 no. 44975 is at Falkirk Grahamston station on 4th March 1964. Photograph by Sid Rickard from the J&J Collection courtesy Rail Photoprints.

FALKLAND JUNCTION – NO. 44319

North of Ayr at Falkland Junction, Fowler 4F Class 0-6-0 no. 44319 has a loaded coal train for Ayr harbour on 23rd June 1961. Photograph by Sid Rickard from the J&J Collection courtesy Rail Photoprints.

Above FORFAR SHED – NO. 54467
Forfar shed sheltered Pickersgill 113 Class no. 54467 between November 1955 and November 1958. The engine is outside the building towards the end of this period. Photograph by Bill Reed.

Below FORFAR STATION – NO. 60034
The 13.30 Aberdeen to Glasgow has made a stop at Forfar station in July 1965. This has allowed no. 60034 *Lord Faringdon* to take on water. Photograph by Brian Robbins courtesy Rail Photoprints.

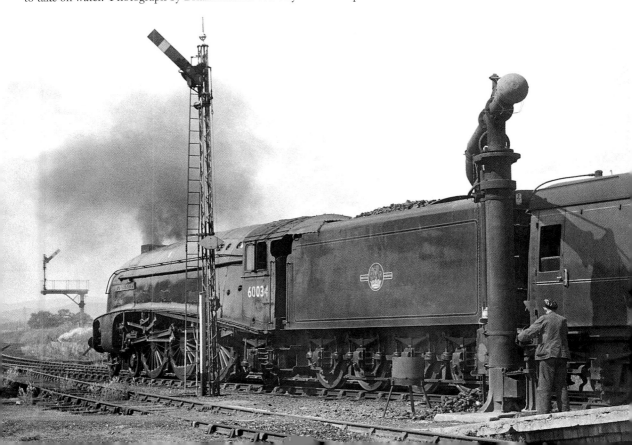

Above FORT WILLIAM STATION – NO. 65313

The difficult terrain and sparse population of the West Highland region deterred railway companies and investors from backing lines there. In the mid-1880s, the scheme was pushed as a right for inhabitants, with some Government funding, and backing from the NBR. The West Highland Railway was started in 1889 and ran from Craigendoran, west of Glasgow, to Fort William via Crianlarich, Rannoch and Spean Bridge. The project was completed in mid-1894, with formal opening on 7th August. Fort William station was established at the edge of Loch Linnhe near the ferry pier to improve links to other areas of western Scotland. Holmes J36 Class no. 65313 has a freight train on the pier line during the 1950s, whilst Stanier Class 5 no. 44974 has a service for Glasgow. Sadly, the original station was replaced by BR in the 1970s. Photograph courtesy Rail-Online.

Opposite above FRASERBURGH SHED – NO. 46460 AND NO. 62276

The Formartine & Buchan Railway opened from Dyce to Peterhead in the early 1860s, followed by an extension to Fraserburgh in the middle of the decade; by the end the line was absorbed into the Great North of Scotland Railway. The original company built an engine shed on the west side of Fraserburgh station and this was in use to 1961 when closed by BR though continues to stand in commercial use. On 17th May 1953 two locomotives are outside the structure, with the station platform canopy seen right. H.G. Ivatt 2MT 2-6-0 no. 46460 is left and was relatively new, being completed at Crewe Works in May 1950 and dispatched to St Margaret's, moving on to Aberdeen Kittybrewster in January 1952. Next to the engine is D40 Class no. 62276 *Andrew Bain*, which also resided at the last mentioned, but was soon to be withdrawn in late August 1955. Photograph courtesy Rail Photoprints.

Opposite below FORT WILLIAM SHED

The Stephenson Locomotive Society organised a railtour from Glasgow Queen Street to Fort William on 18th June 1960. The excursion was led by Gresley K4 Class no. 61995 *Cameron of Lochiel*, which is partially on Fort William depot's turntable here. Also visible is B1 no. 61307 and J36 Class no. 65300. Photograph courtesy Rail Photoprints.

Above GALASHIELS STATION – NO. 65258

Approximately 30 miles from Edinburgh, Galashiels station was opened by the North British Railway in February 1849; later in the year the Waverley route as far as Hawick was ready for traffic. The station was provided with a goods yard at this time owing to the importance of the town to local businesses and several sidings were present, both general and private. Holmes J36 no. 65258 arrives at Galashiels station with a short freight train in the early 1950s – 'British Railways' lettering still adorns the tender. St Margaret's-allocated at this time, the locomotive was condemned there during March 1962. Galashiels station survived to January 1969, when closed to passengers, while freight traffic ceased in April. The route was lifted in the early 1970s. Photograph courtesy Rail-Online.

Opposite GALASHIELS STATION – NO. 61351

Thompson B1 no. 61351 approaches Galashiels station with a local service to Edinburgh on 1st April 1961. The locomotive was amongst a batch of twenty ordered at the end of the LNER, split evenly between the company's workshops at Gorton and Darlington. Some time elapsed before the latter group were completed between July-October 1949. No. 61351 appeared in traffic from Darlington during August 1949 and new to Aberdeen Kittybrewster. Later, in August 1957, a move to Edinburgh occurred and St Margaret's housed the engine to June 1964 when transferred over to Dalry Road depot. Withdrawal happened swiftly after this in July 1964; interestingly, the locomotive's tender at the time was converted into a snow plough. That paired here was not original, as one with countersunk rivets was coupled in 1949. Subsequently, a tender with snaphead rivets has been put in use. Photograph by D.J. Dippie.

Above GIRVAN STATION – NO. 42803 AND NO. 45482

Portpatrick and Stranraer were important points for passengers and cargo crossing between Scotland and Ireland. Only by gradual effort were these points connected from the north and Glasgow. Ayr had been reached in 1840 though another 20 years elapsed before the 20 miles (approx.) between there and Girvan had a line laid. A further 17 passed until Girvan had trains running through to Stranraer owing to the difficult gradients and engineering features necessary. The Girvan & Portpatrick Junction Railway, which completed the work, suffered from operating problems and the line later became part of the Glasgow & South Western Railway. The original station building was a victim of fire in the late 1940s and was rebuilt after Nationalisation. Here, Stanier Class 5 no. 45482 is piloted by Hughes 'Crab' Class no. 42803 with a northbound empty stock working on 13th July 1963 after operating a boat train from Glasgow (see below). The signalman is ready to collect the line staff as this was a single line section. Photograph by Sid Rickard from the J&J Collection courtesy Rail Photoprints.

Opposite GIRVAN STATION – NO. 45482 AND NO. 42803

A busy scene at Girvan station on 13th July 1963. Stanier Class 5 no. 45482 is piloted by Hughes 'Crab' Class no. 42803 on a Glasgow to Stranraer boat train, whilst a mirror of this service approaches in the opposite direction. A DMU is also in sidings on the right. No. 45482 was employed at Grangemouth during the early 1960s and no. 42803 was local to Girvan, being allocated to Ayr depot. The former was withdrawn in 1964 and the latter survived to 1966. Photograph by Sid Rickard from the J&J Collection courtesy Rail Photoprints.

GLASGOW BUCHANAN STREET STATION – NO. 45018
The 09.15 train to Aberdeen from Glasgow Buchanan Street station is at the platform on 30th August 1965, with early Stanier Class 5 no. 45018. Photograph by Geoff Warnes.

Above GLASGOW DAWSHOLM SHED – NO. 43136

Work-worn Ivatt 4MT 2-6-0 no. 43136 is at Dawsholm shed on 6th August 1963. Following just over two years at the depot, the locomotive transferred to Ardsley, near Wakefield. Photograph by D.J. Dippie.

Below GLASGOW POLMADIE SHED – NO. 45700

For fifteen years, Stanier 'Jubilee' Class 4-6-0 no. 45700 ran as *Britannia*. After Nationalisation, this name was chosen for the first BR Standard Class 7 Pacific as part of the 'Festival of Britain' celebrations. The name was removed from no. 45700 in February 1951 and *Amethyst* plates were fitted in September in recognition of the ship from the Royal Navy involved in the 'Yangtze River Incident' during 1949. No. 45700 is at Polmadie shed on 25th September 1955. Photograph by Bill Reed.

GLASGOW POLMADIE SHED – NO. 46250

A pair of Stanier Coronation Class Pacifies is in the yard at Polmadie shed during August 1962 – no. 46250 *City of Lichfield* and no. 46224 *Princess Alexandra*. Photograph by D.J.Dippie.

Above GLASGOW POLMADIE SHED – NO. 76071

Doncaster-built BR Standard Class 4 2-6-0 no. 76071 is at Glasgow Polmadie depot in August 1962. The engine had worked from Motherwell (home from new), though later had a year at Polmadie before condemned in January 1966. Photograph by D.J. Dippie.

Below GLASGOW POLMADIE SHED – NO. 46107

On 21st April 1962, Fowler 'Royal Scot' Class 4-6-0 no. 46107 *Argyll and Sutherland Highlander* is in the yard at Polmadie shed. Photograph by D.J. Dippie.

GLASGOW POLMADIE SHED

A crowded scene outside Polmadie shed on 4th August 1962. There are two BR Standard Class 4 2-6-4Ts, no. 80129 (extreme left) and no. 80054, 'Coronation' Class Pacific no. 46224 *Princess Alexandra*, as well as BR 'Britannia' Class Pacific no. 70052 *Firth of Tay*. Photograph by D.J. Dippie.

Above GLASGOW POLMADIE SHED – NO. 70051

A trio of Pacifics are in line at Polmadie shed on 7th April 1959. At the head is BR 'Britannia' Class Pacific no. 70051 *Firth of Forth*, which was one of six class members named after Firths. Photograph by Bill Reed.

Below GLASGOW POLMADIE SHED – NO. 76000

The Ivatt Class 4MT 2-6-0 was the basis for the BR Standard Class 4 which was mainly used on freight duties. No. 76000 was the first to be built and was sent from Horwich Works to Motherwell shed in December 1952. The engine remained in service there through to withdrawal in May 1967. A total of 115 were constructed and four were subsequently preserved. Photograph courtesy Rail Photoprints.

Above GLASGOW BUCHANAN STREET STATION – NO. 72008

A slightly smaller version of the BR Standard Class 7 Pacific was built to increase the route availability. This was the Standard Class 6 and ten were built initially, mostly for service in Scotland. As a result, all were named after Clans, particularly following the recent withdrawal of a Highland Railway class bearing such names. No. 72008 *Clan MacLeod* entered traffic from Crewe Works and was new to Carlisle Kingmoor (for a time in the 1950s, the depot was part of the Scottish Region) and this proved the sole allocation. The locomotive is at Glasgow Buchanan Street station with an express in 1956. Photograph from the John Day Collection courtesy Rail Photoprints.

Opposite GLASGOW ST ENOCH STATION – NO. 45463

An Ayrshire coast express is at Glasgow St Enoch station on 24th July 1961. The City of Glasgow Union Railway was conceived to connect all the lines entering the area in the early 1860s. Several companies were operating at the time, though not all expressed an interest, likely due to the high cost. Nevertheless, the line, which crossed the Clyde, was ready for freight traffic in September 1870, followed by passenger services at the end of the year. As part of the project, a central station was built at St Enoch Square, yet this did not open until 1876, consisting of six platforms covered by a glass canopy 504 ft long, spanning 198 ft and 80 ft above the ground. Originally operating under the City of Glasgow Union Railway, the Glasgow & South Western Railway later took over the facility and the company's trains ran there, along with the Midland Railway from England. St Enoch station operated to 1966 when a victim of Dr Beeching and later demolished. Stanier Class 5 no. 45463 was similarly a victim of 'modernisation' in late 1966. At the time of the picture, the engine was Ardrossan-allocated – a '67D' shed plate is fitted. Photograph by Sid Rickard from the J&J Collection courtesy Rail Photoprints.

Above GLASGOW ST ENOCH STATION – NO. 80004

A number of BR Standard Class 4 2-6-4T locomotives were to replace life-expired classes in Northern Scotland, as well as in suburban areas, particularly Glasgow. The first ten from Derby Works were selected to go, yet delays saw ten from Brighton to be the first in country beginning October 1951. The initial allocation was sent to work from September 1952 and no. 80004 was amongst these, reporting for duty at Aberdeen Kittybrewster in November. By 1963, the engine was in Glasgow, firstly at Eastfield, then Dawsholm briefly before reaching Corkerhill in late 1964. No. 80004 has the depot's '67A' shed code here at St Enoch station on 28th August 1965. At the end of steam in the Scottish Region – 1st May 1967 – no. 80004 was one of the final locomotives in service, though was subsequently scrapped. Photograph by Geoff Warnes.

Opposite GLASGOW ST ENOCH STATION – NO. 44718

A large number of Stanier Class 5 4-6-0s were erected between 1935 and 1951. At the latter date, 842 locomotives had been built to the design at several locations. The specifications for the engines were not static, however, and evolved a number of times, with some of these being for a small batch or others perpetuated on a large number. No. 44718 was ordered as part of Lot no. 192 in October 1946. Consisting of 40 Class 5s, the task was split between Crewe and Horwich Works, with no. 44718 the product of the first mentioned in March 1949. The first ten of the order built at Crewe possessed steel inner fireboxes which were fitted due to Scotland being the destined sphere of operation and owing to the soft water in use there. The application proved successful in these locomotives but not extended to other class members. One other change for no. 44718 onwards was the use of standard return loop superheater elements 1⅜ in. diameter and 9 swg thick. No. 44718 was new to Carlisle Kingmoor shed and in 1952 transferred to Inverness, spending nearly ten years at work there. The locomotive is pictured on 21st April 1962 when Hurlford-based and perhaps has a local train for Kilmarnock here. At the next platform is Stanier 'Jubilee' Class no. 45729 *Furious*, which was a Kingmoor engine. Photograph by D.J. Dippie.

GLASGOW ST ENOCH STATION

Two BR Standard Class 4 2-6-4T engines are at the head of respective local services from St Enoch station on 31st July 1961. Left is no. 80052 and right is no. 80048. Photograph by D.J. Dippie.

Above GLASGOW ST ENOCH STATION – NO. 42190

Water is filled into the tank of Fairburn 4P Class 2-6-4T no. 42190 at St Enoch station on 31st July 1960. The locomotive was new from Derby just after Nationalisation and the first allocation was to Corkerhill depot. The engine's only time away was six months at Plaistow, East London, from mid-1951 to early 1952. Photograph by D.J. Dippie.

Below GLASGOW ST ENOCH STATION – NO. 80052

BR Standard Class 4 2-6-4T no. 80052 is leaving St Enoch station on 31st July 1961. Unlike other class members, no. 80052 was not new in Scotland and spent time in the North West before transfer to Corkerhill in 1960. Photograph by D.J. Dippie.

Above GLASGOW ST ROLLOX WORKS – NO. 56025 AND NO. 44954
A short distance east of Buchanan Street station, the Caledonian Railway established locomotive construction and repair facilities at St Rollox. The area went on to be heavily industrialised, with the NBR's Cowlairs Works, North British Locomotive Company's two shops, to the north west and north respectively, as well as steel and chemical works nearby. Covering 15 acres (approx.), St Rollox concentrated on repairs following takeover by the London Midland & Scottish Railway after Grouping and continued in this capacity through the BR period. Drummond 264 Class 0-4-0ST no. 56025 is pictured on 31st May 1951 and has brought Stanier Class 5 no. 44954 out of the works after a repair has been carried out. Photograph by George C. Lander courtesy Rail Photoprints.

Opposite above GLASGOW ST ROLLOX SHED – NO. 90493
View eastward along the mainline from Stirling, etc., to Buchanan Street station on 5th October 1961. WD 'Austerity' Class no. 90493 is approaching Broomfield Road bridge with a mixed freight train featuring a new diesel-electric shunter, D4098. This latter had been recently constructed at Horwich Works and the first allocation was to Perth in early September. No. 90493 was built at Vulcan Foundry in August 1944 and saw service in France with the US Army. When repatriated, the engine was bought by the LNER and used in Scotland. Between December 1951 and August 1962, no. 90493 worked from Dawsholm. The train is passing St Rollox depot and the coal stage, with several locomotives being serviced. In the line, from left to right, are: Stanier Class 5 no. 44922; Peppercorn A2 Pacific no. 60527 *Sun Chariot*; 4F 0-6-0 no. 44312; unidentified CR 0-6-0. Stanier Class 5 no. 45360 is behind the diesel shunter. Photograph by B.W.L. Brooksbank.

Opposite below GLASGOW ST ROLLOX WORKS – NO. 56025
Dugald Drummond introduced his 264 Class 0-4-0ST design in 1885 for shunting work mainly around Glasgow. Eight were built initially, followed by two batches of six before he left the Caledonian Railway in 1890. Later examples numbered 14 and completed under J.F. McIntosh. No. 56025 was the last of the class built under Drummond, entering service from St Rollox Works in May 1890 as CR no. 515. Subsequently, the locomotive had long-term employment as works shunter at St Rollox and is outside the shops here in late 1948. The BR number was applied from August and the company has also branded the engine. Withdrawal occurred in May 1960. Photograph courtesy Rail Online.

Above GLENFARG – NO. 61993

The NBR's lines ran into the Highlands, reaching Fort William and Mallaig and offered particular challenges of gradients, also weather conditions. In 1923, traffic on the line was operated by D34s, latterly in pairs, owing to increased weight of coaching stock. Gresley K2 Class 2-6-0s also assisted on the route after being replaced on the GN Section. In the mid-1930s, further consideration was given to the challenges of the line and a new 2-6-0 was designed. One K4 was ordered initially and built at Darlington in 1937. This was no. 61993 *Loch Long*, as LNER no. 3441, and the engine worked from Glasgow Eastfield to May 1959 when displaced to Thornton Junction shed. No. 61993 is pictured later in the year working a train of empty coal wagons on Glenfarg bank (south of Perth). The locomotive was condemned in October 1961. Photograph by W.J. Verden Anderson from Rail Archive Stephenson courtesy Rail-Online.

Opposite GLENEAGLES – NO. 61398

The Scottish Central Railway was promoted in the mid-1840s to connect Perth and Stirling with Glasgow. The company joined both the Edinburgh & Glasgow Railway and Caledonian Railway, with a junction made west of Falkirk. The SCR later amalgamated with the latter in 1865. The line passed through Gleneagles (south west of Perth) and this later became the departure point for the Crieff branch, opened in 1856. The station there was first called Crieff Junction, though later became Gleneagles in 1912. Nearby, the CR began a project to build a hotel resort and golf course which was completed in the mid-1920s. Thompson B1 no. 61398 travels through the area with a mixed freight train of goods vans and coal wagons on 4th September 1964. Just two months in traffic remained for the locomotive and a move to Dundee Tay Bridge depot had occurred recently. No. 61398 had been a Scottish engine from new in March 1952; construction was carried out by the NBLC. Photograph from the Dave Cobbe Collection courtesy Rail Photoprints.

Above GREENHILL STATION – NO. 90386

WD 'Austerity' no. 90386 passes Greenhill station with a brake van on 7th September 1966. Closure had occurred in April after 118 years serving the area from opening by the Scottish Central Railway. No. 90386 survived almost to the end of steam in Scotland and worked from Dunfermline for much of the mid-1960s. Photograph by David Christie.

Opposite above GLENOGLE – NO. 45178

The Callander & Oban Railway stalled at Glenogle in 1870 and a station was built for the nearby Killin. Progress was made in 1873 when the next section to Tyndrum was completed. The station remained and was later renamed Glenoglehead when a branch to Killin opened in 1886, but closure to passengers came at the end of the decade. Yet, the site became a passing point for trains on the single-track route, as well as the place of exchange for the signal token. Stanier Class 5 no. 45178 is about to make the swap on 22nd August 1960. The train originated at Oban and was destined for Glasgow. Photograph by Hugh Ballantyne courtesy Rail Photoprints.

Opposite below GRANGEMOUTH – NO. 90757

In addition to the War Department 'Austerity' 2-8-0, a 2-10-0 version of the design was built. A wide firebox took the place of the narrow type fitted to the former and the extra wheelset provided greater route availability. A comparatively small number were built between 1943 and 1945 – 150 – and many saw use on the continent, with a large amount later taken into stock by the Netherlands. Just 25 were in service under BR. No. 90757 was completed by the NBLC at the end of the war and was later loaned to the LNER. After a time in storage, the engine was bought by BR and later allocated for work in the Scottish Region at Grangemouth. No. 90757 has a freight train there on 27th September 1957. The locomotive was sent for scrap in December 1962. Photograph by B.W.L. Brooksbank.

Above GRESKINE – NO. 45122

Ascending Beattock bank at Greskine, Stanier Class 5 no. 45122 is assisted on a freight train by Fairburn 4P Class no. 42192 during October 1963. No. 45122 appears to have been worked hard by Carlisle Kingmoor depot and was to only survive another six months. No. 42192 was at Beattock shed for work as a banker but was similarly dismissed in early 1964. Photograph by Hugh Ballantyne courtesy Rail Photoprints.

Opposite above GREENLOANING STATION – NO. 57232

An early CR Drummond 294 Class 0-6-0 is pictured at Greenloaning station during the 1950s. The latter was to close during the decade (1956) and had been opened by the Scottish Central Railway in 1848. No. 57232, which is leading a mixed freight train, appeared in service from Neilson, Reid & Co. in November 1883 as the third class member of an eventual total of 244, with variations from other engineers. The locomotive worked for BR at Stirling depot and was condemned there during May 1961. Photograph courtesy Rail-Online.

Opposite below GREENHILL STATION – NO. 65923

Gresley J38 Class no. 65923 takes the goods loop around Greenhill station on 19th September 1957. The engine was a long-term resident of Dunfermline shed, arriving there in December 1943 and working to December 1962. Duties for J38s at the depot included goods trains on the main routes, in addition to trip coal trains. Photograph by B.W.L. Brooksbank.

HAWICK – NO. 60131
An Edinburgh Millerhill to Leeds freight train
is at Hawick behind Peppercorn A1 Class Pacific
no. 60131 *Osprey* on 29th July 1964. Photograph
from Norman Preedy Archive courtesy Rail
Photoprints.

Above HOOKHILLS CUTTING – NO. 67615

Climbing southward through Hookhills cutting to the Forth Bridge, Gresley V3 no. 67615 has a local train from Dunfermline to Edinburgh on 27th April 1957. Photograph by David Anderson courtesy Rail Photoprints.

Below HAMILTONHILL – NO. 45100

Stanier Class 5 no. 45100 is on the freight only branch at Hamiltonhill around 1963. Photograph by Sid Rickard from the J&J Collection courtesy Rail Photoprints.

Above HAWICK STATION – NO. 60079

The 14.36 Edinburgh Waverley to Carlisle local, with Gresley A3 Pacific no. 60079 *Bayardo*, pauses at Hawick station to collect passengers on 26th August 1960. Photograph by Hugh Ballantyne courtesy Rail Photoprints.

Below HEADS OF AYR STATION – NO. 45491

Heads of Ayr station served a local Butlins holiday camp. Stanier Class 5 no. 45491 has an 08.35 train to Leeds on 24th June 1961. Photograph by Sid Rickard from the J&J Collection courtesy Rail Photoprints.

Above INVERKEITHING STATION – NO. 44931

A train from Perth to Edinburgh has reached Inverkeithing station on 26th August 1965 behind well-presented Class 5 no. 44931. Photograph by David Christie.

Below HURLFORD SHED – NO. 42739

Hughes 'Crab' Class no. 42739 is outside Hurlford shed on 24th April 1966. The engine survived to the end of the year. Photograph by Bill Wright.

Below INVERKEITHING – NO. 60024

View north at Inverkeithing to the junction for the line east to Burntisland, Thornton Junction, Dundee, etc., and west to Dunfermline, Stirling and Alloa. Gresley A4 Class Pacific no. 60024 *Kingfisher* is near Inverkeithing Central Junction signal box light engine on 4th September 1966. This was the engine's last day in service and saw use on the South and West Railway Society's 'Granite City' railtour from Aberdeen to Edinburgh. No. 60024 had recently acquired streamlined non-corridor tender no. 5640 from the withdrawn no. 60034 *Lord Faringdon*, whilst the previously used corridor type, no. 5329, was condemned with the latter. Photograph by David Christie.

Above INVERKEITHING – NO. 61147

A local train is Edinburgh-bound at Inverkeithing on 20th June 1959. The locomotive employed is Thompson B1 no. 61147. In January 1946, the LNER ordered 200 of the class, with 150 from the NBLC and 50 from Vulcan Foundry. No. 61147 was the product of the latter in April 1947 and was new in Scotland to Aberdeen Kittybrewster. As a result, the locomotive was soon after fitted with tablet exchange apparatus. A move to Dundee occurred in the early 1950s then Thornton Junction, where no. 61147 remained until 1965. The depot's duties mainly consisted of local services in the area and to Edinburgh and Glasgow. Photograph by David Anderson courtesy Rail Photoprints.

Above INVERKEITHING – NO. 64569

Reid J37 no. 64569 approaches Inverkeithing East Junction with a holiday train bound for Aberdour in 1957. Photograph by David Anderson courtesy Rail Photoprints.

Below INVERKEITHING – NO. 62427

The 13.45 from Stirling, via Alloa and Dunfermline, is at Inverkeithing station and bound for Edinburgh on 19th September 1957. The engine is Reid D30 no. 62427 *Dumbiedykes*. Photograph by B.W.L. Brooksbank.

Above INVERNESS – NO. 17954

Ex-HR Cumming 'Clan Goods' Class 4-6-0 no. 17954 is present in this panoramic view of the goods yard east of Inverness station on 23rd August 1948. The locomotive, which is fitted with a tablet catcher, was in service to October 1952 when condemned as BR no. 57594. Photograph by B.W.L. Brooksbank.

Below INVERNESS SHED – NO. 16293

In the yard at Inverness shed on 22nd August 1948 is McIntosh 782 Class 0-6-0T no. 16293. The locomotive's shed plate is fitted at the top of the smokebox door. This bears the '32A' shed code of Inverness under the LMSR, though this later became '60A' for BR. Photograph by B.W.L. Brooksbank.

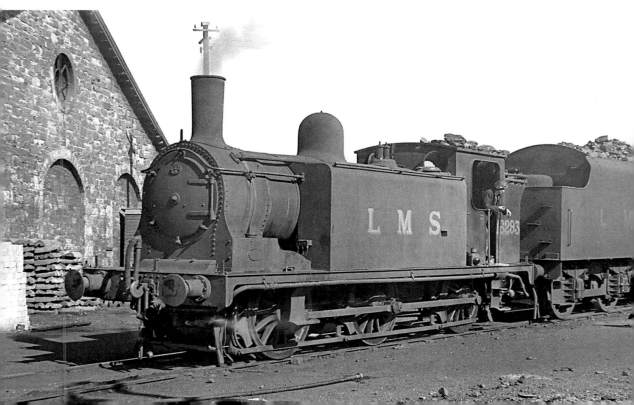

Above KENTALLEN – NO. 57571

South west of Ballachulish at Kentallen, McIntosh 812 Class 0-6-0 no. 57571 has a mixed freight destined for Oban in August 1960. The engine was based at the latter place from July 1958 to October 1961 and moved on to Polmadie. Six months later, no. 57571 was sent for scrap. Photograph courtesy Rail Photoprints.

Opposite above INVERKEITHING – NO. 64636

A Sunday school excursion from Anstruther passes through Inverkeithing on the way to Edinburgh during 1961. Reid J37 Class no. 64636 leads the party and was Polmont-allocated at the time, suggesting the engine has been pressed into service. Built at Cowlairs Works in August 1921, no. 64636 was condemned at Grangemouth in October 1964. Photograph by David Anderson courtesy Rail Photoprints.

Opposite below KILMARNOCK STATION – NO. 45621

A horse-drawn railway started Kilmarnock's association with the transport when the Kilmarnock & Troon Railway opened on 6th July 1812 for goods, then 1818 for passengers. This later upgraded to use a steam locomotive and the next project saw the town linked with Ayr in 1839. The Glasgow, Paisley, Kilmarnock & Ayr Railway opened the station in early April 1843. Stanier 'Jubilee' Class no. 45621 *Northern Rhodesia* appears to have a parcels train at Kilmarnock station on 26th June 1961. The engine was working from Corkerhill at the time and in December 1962 was withdrawn from there. Photograph by Bill Reed.

KIRKCALDY – NO. 62691
Robinson D11/2 no. 62691 *Laird of Balmawhapple* has reached Kirkcaldy with an Edinburgh to Dundee train during July 1950. Photograph by George C. Lander courtesy Rail Photoprints.

Above KILMARNOCK STATION – NO. 45742
An express unfitted freight, with containers behind the tender, passes through Kilmarnock station behind Stanier 'Jubilee' no. 45742 *Connaught* on 7th May 1963. Photograph by Bill Reed.

Below KILLIN STATION – NO. 55263
The Killin branch train is ready to depart for Killin Junction on 22nd August 1960. McIntosh 2P 0-4-4T no. 55263 is the locomotive. Photograph by Hugh Ballantyne courtesy Rail Photoprints.

Left KINCARDINE POWER STATION
– NO. 65903

On the north bank of the Firth of Forth, just west of Kincardine, the South of Scotland Electricity Board established a new power station in the early 1950s. This generated 760 MW and was to supply one-third of Scotland's energy requirements when commissioned in 1958. Coal was constantly supplied from the local fields, while there were also storage sidings and facilities for engines working on site. Gresley J38 Class no. 65903 is leaving the power station with empty coal wagons in August 1966. Photograph by Dave Swale courtesy Rail Photoprints.

Below KILWINNING STATION
– NO. 42190

East of Ardrossan, Fairburn 4P Class no. 42190 has a southbound freight on the line to Ayr/Stranraer during mid-September 1957. Photograph by B.W.L. Brooksbank.

Above KIPPS – NO. 68110
Drummond Y9 Class 0-4-0ST no. 68110 had been withdrawn from service for two months when pictured at Kipps shed on 5th October 1961. Photograph by B.W.L. Brooksbank.

Below LANARK STATION – NO. 45168
A short local train is to travel the equally short distance between Lanark and Carstairs on 21st September 1963. Stanier Class 5 no. 45168 is at the head of the formation. Photograph by Sid Rickard from the J&J Collection courtesy Rail Photoprints.

Above LANARK STATION – NO. 77019

BR introduced the Standard Class 3 2-6-0 to cover lines restricting the use of Class 4s, whilst the coupling of a tender provided an advantage over the range of tank engines that might otherwise have been employed. Just 20 were built at Swindon Works in 1954, with no. 77019 being the last in traffic during September. The class was spread between the Scottish Region and the North Eastern Region, with no. 77019 allocated to Hurlford, near Kilmarnock. Duties for the Class 3s included trains to Glasgow, Dumfries, Ayr and Lanark, both passenger and freight. A passenger train from Kilmarnock to Lanark via Muirkirk has brought no. 77019 to Lanark station here c. 1960. Photograph courtesy Rail-Online.

Opposite above LARGS STATION – NO. 45488

During the mid-1860s, the Glasgow & South Western Railway began a project to connect the coastal town of Largs with the system. The line was to leave Dalry at this time, though opposition forced the project to be dropped. In the early 1870s, the G&SWR changed the route to leave Ardrossan northward to West Kilbride and this connection was made at the end of the decade, followed by another section to Fairlie. Nearly 20 years after the original proposal, Largs saw the first train arrive in 1885. Stanier Class 5 no. 45488 is at the station with a local train to Glasgow on 21st April 1962. Largs station remains open and has been completely rebuilt. Photograph by Sid Rickard from the J&J Collection courtesy Rail Photoprints.

Opposite below LARBERT STATION – NO. 42198

Larbert station opened with the Scottish Central Railway in 1848. Later, the station was between several junctions, including those to Alloa, Falkirk, Denny and Grangemouth. Fairburn 4P Class no. 42198 has a local train for the latter at Larbert during the mid- to late 1950s. The locomotive was built at Derby Works in March 1948 and new to Stirling depot. After 12 years, a transfer to the London Midland Region occurred and Chester received the engine. Photograph courtesy Rail-Online.

LEUCHARS JUNCTION STATION – NO. 64569
The 'Fife Coast' railtour was organised by the RCTS on 28th
August 1965. Between Leuchars Junction and Thornton Junction
Reid J37 no. 64569 was the engine employed. Photograph by
Geoff Warnes.

Above LEUCHARS JUNCTION STATION – NO. 61103
Leuchars Junction was where the line northward split to Tayport or for the Tay Bridge, with a connection on this westward, eventually reaching Perth. Thompson B1 no. 61103 has an excursion train for the Fife Coast at the station on 16th July 1955. Photograph courtesy Rail-Online.

Below LOCKERBIE STATION – NO. 70037
A milk train from Lockerbie is bound for Glasgow in July 1965 behind BR 'Britannia' no. 70037 *Hereward the Wake*. Note the road/rail tanker in the formation. Photograph by Derek Cross courtesy Rail Photoprints.

MAWCARSE – NO. 60534

The 16.05 train from Edinburgh to Perth is at Mawcarse in the 1950s with Peppercorn A2 no. 60534 *Irish Elegance*. Photograph by W.J. Verden Anderson from Rail Archive Stephenson courtesy Rail-Online.

Above LOSSIEMOUTH STATION – NO. 78053
An Elgin to Lossiemouth train has reached the latter station in the 1950s with BR Standard Class 2 2-6-0 no. 78053. Photograph courtesy Rail-Online.

Below MAXTON STATION – NO. 64917
A Tweedmouth to St Boswells freight passes through Maxton station on 26th August 1960. Gresley J39 Class no. 64917 is the engine. Photograph by Hugh Ballantyne courtesy Rail Photoprints.

Above METHIL – NO. 19

An extensive railway network was developed to serve the collieries operated on lands in Fife belonging to local Laird Randolph Wemyss. This became known as the Wemyss Private Railway and ran along much of the south east coast of Fife between East Wemyss and Methil and Leven, the latter two being developed as ports for the export of coal traffic. Leven was the primary point of departure originally, though the NBR promoted Burntisland as the main port to incur extra costs of transport. Methil subsequently took the role due to the more advantageous site and up to 3,000,000 tons were moved through there during the inter-war years. On 6th January 1970, Andrew Barclay 0-6-0T no. 19 (works no. 2067) is at Methil with a load of coal for the washer at Wellesley colliery, south of the dock. The locomotive had been purchased just before the Second World War to work on the Wemyss Private Railway and was amongst the last in service when closure occurred in June 1970. No. 19 was scrapped later in the year. Photograph by David P. Williams courtesy Rail-Online.

Opposite below MOTHERWELL STATION – NO. 57568

A wintry scene captured at Motherwell station on 8th February 1963 as McIntosh 812 Class no. 57568 passes through with a brake van. Photograph by Sid Rickard from the J&J Collection courtesy Rail Photoprints.

Above MOTHERWELL – NO. 46255

Stanier 'Coronation' Pacific no. 46255 *City of Hereford* departs from Motherwell station with a Euston to Perth express on 28th March 1963. The engine was working from Carlisle Kingmoor at the time and condemned at the depot in September 1964. Photograph by Sid Rickard from the J&J Collection courtesy Rail Photoprints.

Above NEWTON-ON-AYR STATION – NO. 42742

George Hughes was CME of the London & North Western Railway at Grouping and only briefly held the same position with the LMSR, retiring in 1925. In this short period, he produced the mixed traffic 2-6-0 or 'Crab' Class design which went on to number 245 examples across the system. No. 42742 was the product of Crewe Works early in the programme, entering traffic during March 1927 and being in service to July 1962. The locomotive has been pictured with a short freight train at Newton-on-Ayr station on 22nd June 1961. Photograph by Sid Rickard from the J&J Collection courtesy Rail Photoprints.

Opposite above NEW CUMNOCK – NO. 73120 AND NO. 45126

Between Kilmarnock and Dumfries at New Cumnock on the ex-GSWR line a troop special has been captured on 4th July 1966. The regiment on board is the Household Cavalry and horseboxes are included centrally between the passenger carriages. BR Standard Class 5 no. 73120 is piloting Stanier Class 5 no. 45126 on the train which originated at Glasgow and bound for Kensington Olympia. The first mentioned was allocated to Corkerhill depot, whilst no. 45126 had employment at Carlisle Kingmoor. Photograph by Derek Cross courtesy Rail Photoprints.

Opposite below MUSSELBURGH – NO. 67630

The station for Musselburgh (on the Firth of Forth, east of Edinburgh) was originally on the NBR main line when built in 1846, yet a branch to the centre of the town was laid in the following year. This was open to 1964 and lasted to 1970 for freight. During the late 1980s, a new station was again established on the main line. Gresley V1 Class 2-6-2T no. 67630 has the 12.49 local train to Edinburgh Waverley set to depart from Musselburgh on 15th July 1955. Under BR, the locomotive was mainly at St Margaret's depot, apart from a short spell at Hawick in 1956 and the early 1960s saw no. 67630 in Glasgow at Eastfield and Parkhead. Withdrawal occurred at the end of 1962. Photograph courtesy Rail-Online.

Opposite above NORTH QUEENSFERRY
– NO. 61721

Gresley K2 Class 2-6-0 no. 61721 is about to cross the Forth Bridge from North Queensferry on 27th June 1956. Built for the Great Northern Railway in February 1913, the locomotive's early career was based in Nottingham at Colwick shed, then under the LNER, several depots in the Great Eastern Section retained no. 61721's services. In the 1920s and 1930s, several class members had been transferred to the West Highland line, though no. 61721 was a late arrival in Scotland and was sent instead to Dunfermline. The engine has a train from there to Glasgow. Photograph by David Anderson courtesy Rail Photoprints.

Opposite below OBAN – NO. 78052

BR Standard Class 2 no. 78052 is at Oban shed on 6th August 1962. Photograph by Neville Simms from the Ranwell Collection courtesy Rail Photoprints.

Below OAKLEY – NO. 65288

Around halfway between Alloa and Dunfermline, the village of Oakley had a station on the line connecting the two places, in addition to a branch for a local colliery. Just before the war, a new pit was sunk, Comrie colliery. Sidings for the output were laid in the 1950s a short distance off the main line on the branch. Holmes J36 Class no. 65288 is at Oakley on 8th September 1966. Despite being 70 years old, the locomotive worked on for another year. Photograph by David Christie.

Above OBAN – NO. 55208

As the line from Connel Ferry rounded into Oban from the south a split was made to reach the goods station to the east and the terminus in the north west side of the town. Between the two lines, an engine shed and servicing facilities were installed by the Callander & Oban Railway in 1880. McIntosh 439 Class 0-4-4T no. 55208 is pictured at the depot from Glenshellach Terrace on 21st September 1957. The engine transferred from Perth to Oban in May 1955 and served there to July 1961 when condemned for scrap. The locomotive depot continued to May 1963. Photograph by B.W.L. Brooksbank.

Opposite above OBAN – NO. 55226 AND NO. 55195

View northward from Glenshellach Road to Oban shed and the goods station beyond during August 1960. Closest to the camera and in storage are two identified McIntosh 439 Class 0-4-4T locomotives, no. 55226 and no. 55195, and another which is unrecorded. Both aforementioned were not Oban-allocated at this time, with Perth and Stirling respectively having the locomotives on their rosters. Photograph courtesy Rail Photoprints.

Opposite below PAISLEY GILMOUR STREET STATION – NO. 42259

Two railway companies came together to open a joint station at Paisley in the late 1830s. The Glasgow, Paisley & Greenock and Glasgow, Paisley, Kilmarnock & Ayr Railways laid a single line from Glasgow to Paisley where they split to reach their respective destinations. Gilmour Street station was opened in 1840, with the last mentioned company advanced enough to begin running trains, whilst the other was not ready until the following year. Fairburn 4P Class no. 42259 has the 12.08 Glasgow to Gourock train on 4th January 1965. At the west end of the station, the line to Kilmarnock and Ayr branches off to the left. Photograph by Sid Rickard from the J&J Collection courtesy Rail Photoprints.

PERTH – NO. 73151

On the southern approach to Perth, BR Standard Class 5 no. 73151 is about to enter Moncrieffe tunnel with an express on 25th August 1965. The engine was one of thirty class members with British Caprotti valve gear and poppet valves. Photograph by David Christie.

Above PERTH SHED – NO. 44703

Stanier Class 5 no. 44703 is at Perth shed on 25th August 1965. Aberdeen Ferryhill-allocated at this time, the engine was there for another year and briefly transferred to Glasgow Eastfield before condemned. Photograph by David Christie.

Below PERTH – NO. 44998

On 30th August 1965, Stanier Class 5 no. 44998 has the 'Granite City' express at Perth. The engine was a long-term servant at the local shed. Photograph by Geoff Warnes.

Above PERTH, HILTON JUNCTION – NO. 73146

Members of a track gang are interrupted by BR Standard Class 5 no. 73146 approaching Hilton Junction, south of Perth, on 28th April 1964. The train is a Dundee to Glasgow, via Perth, express, which is taking the ex-Scottish Central Railway line via Dunblane, Stirling, etc. The line branching off to the right is the ex-NBR line to Mawcarse, Kinross, Alloa, etc., as well as Dundee, Ladybank, Thornton Junction, etc. No. 73146 was another Class 5 fitted from new with British Caprotti valve gear and poppet valves. This system, in several forms, had been tested on a number of classes from the 1930s and BR made another experiment after Nationalisation. Costing some £6,000 more than a standard engine, the Caprotti gear showed a 25% increase in longevity over piston valves, in addition to providing more accurate valve events. Though noted as 'sluggish' at slower speeds, free-running at high speed was an advantage. Photograph by Revd J. David Benson courtesy A1 Steam Trust.

Above PERTH SHED – NO. 44978 AND NO. 44959

On 16th July 1965, a pair of decommissioned Stanier Class 5 locomotives are at Perth shed. No. 44978 is nearest and had been condemned a week earlier, as had no. 44959; both are equipped with tablet exchange apparatus. Photograph by Bill Wright.

Below PERTH SHED – NO. 54500

Pickersgill 72 Class 4-4-0 no. 54500 is in the yard at Perth shed in the late 1950s. The engine was at the depot throughout the BR period and was condemned there in March 1962. Photograph by Bill Reed.

Above PERTH SHED – NO. 60006 AND NO. 60009

A4s no. 60006 *Sir Ralph Wedgwood* and no. 60009 *Union of South Africa* are in the yard at Perth shed on 18th July 1965. None was allocated to the depot, mainly working from Aberdeen Ferryhill, with a pair – no. 60027 and 60031 – at Glasgow St Rollox. No. 60006 was at Aberdeen from May 1964 and in service there for over a year until condemned in September 1965. No. 60009 was at Haymarket from new, then went north to Ferryhill in May 1962 and was amongst the last A4s in traffic, later being preserved. Photograph by Bill Wright.

Opposite PERTH STATION – NO. 60034

Gresley A4 Pacific no. 60034 *Lord Faringdon* was the final class member in traffic during July 1938 bringing the total to 35. The three of the final A4s were equipped with Kylchap double blastpipes and chimneys which improved performance. No. 60034, as LNER no. 4903, was new to Doncaster shed and during the war moved on to King's Cross, then soon after Grantham. *Lord Faringdon* returned to King's Cross in 1948 and became one of the depot's top performers during the 1950s, working many of the East Coast Main Line's premier trains. In October 1963, the engine was allocated to St Margaret's and six months later moved to Aberdeen Ferryhill. No. 60034 is pictured here working the 17.15 Aberdeen to Glasgow express on 18th July 1966. Taking water at Perth, *Lord Faringdon* had used a corridor tender for most of the 1950s, though had received streamlined non-corridor tender no. 5640 in early 1963. Photograph by Bill Wright.

Above PORT GLASGOW STATION – NO. 80002

The Glasgow, Paisley & Greenock Railway opened Port Glasgow station with the line in 1841 and the facility is still in operation. BR Standard Class 4 no. 80002 has paused at the station with a local train to Gourock on 6th July 1965. Polmadie-allocated at this time, the engine was withdrawn there in March 1967. Photograph by John Vaughan courtesy Rail Photoprints.

Opposite above POLMONT SHED – NO. 65275

East of Falkirk on the Edinburgh-Glasgow line, Polmont shed was a late addition, being constructed by the NBR in 1914. This was perhaps due to the sinking of Meadowbank colliery immediately adjacent, as well as associated sidings, which were to the west of Polmont station and near the junction with the line to Stirling and Alloa. Holmes J36 Class no. 65275 is leaving the depot yard on 27th September 1957. The engine had been employed at Polmont for a number of years, but a transfer to Hawick approached in 1958. No. 65275 returned briefly in early 1962, then was condemned at Grangemouth in December of the year. Photograph by B.W.L. Brooksbank.

Opposite below POLMONT SHED – NO. 69014

Worsdell J72 Class 0-6-0T no. 69014 stands at the head of a line of stored locomotives at Polmont shed on 30th August 1960. St Margaret's '64A' shed plate is on the smokebox door and the engine returned to work there subsequently, though later returned to store in 1961 and was condemned in 1962. Photograph by D.J. Dippie.

Above POLMONT SHED – NO. 64571

Reid J37 Class no. 64571 survived the closure of Polmont shed – a long-term residence – and was taken on at Grangemouth, then Dunfermline to withdrawal in October 1965. The locomotive had been new from the NBLC in August 1918. In front of no. 64571 is W. Worsdell J72 Class 0-6-0T no. 69014. The engine belonged to an NER design which was perpetuated after Nationalisation and construction was carried out at Darlington in late 1949. Photograph by D.J. Dippie.

Opposite above POLMONT SHED – NO. 68354

The shed at Polmont was constructed from wood and possessed five tracks. In the mid-1950s, the allocation consisted mainly of freight types numbering 42: 24 0-6-0s; 6 0-6-0Ts; 2 2-6-0s; 5 4-4-2T; 3 0-6-2T; 2 0-4-0T. Outside the shed on 27th September 1957 is Reid J88 Class 0-6-0T no. 68354, which was mainly allocated to Polmont under BR with two short loans to Kipps in late 1957 and early 1960. At the end of the latter, the locomotive was withdrawn for scrap. Reid J36 Class no. 65275 is also present (see p. 133). Polmont shed closed in May 1964. Photograph by B.W.L. Brooksbank.

Opposite below POLMONT SHED – NO. 67494

Several locomotives are pictured in storage at Polmont shed on 30th August 1960. At the head of the line is Reid C16 Class 4-4-2T no. 67494. The locomotive was one of twenty-one built to the design by the NBLC and was a superheated version of the earlier C15 (NBR L and M Classes respectively). The type also possessed piston valves. No. 67494 was erected during April 1916 and in traffic to February 1961. From October 1953 to the latter date, the engine was Polmont-allocated. Standing behind the C16 is no. 68471 which belonged to the Holmes J83 Class. Built by Sharp, Stewart & Co. in April 1901, the locomotive survived just longer than no. 67494, being removed from duty in August 1961. Under BR no. 68471 was at Polmont. Photograph by D.J. Dippie.

Below RIDDOCHHILL COLLIERY
– NO. 65234

A mineral branch line left the main line at Bathgate and went southward to Riddochhill colliery. Holmes J36 Class no. 65234 is pictured there shunting coal wagons on 10th August 1964. The engine worked from Bathgate at this time and a month later moved on to serve at St Margaret's to the end of steam when 75 years old. Photograph courtesy Rail Photoprints.

Above ROBROYSTON – NO. 44998

Under BR, several named trains ran between Glasgow and Aberdeen on the ex-CR lines. One was the 'Bon Accord' which was the early morning Aberdeen to Glasgow train that, in the late 1940s, left at 06.25, though was accelerated in the 1960s and rescheduled to 07.10. Stanier Class 5 no. 44998 has the train at Robroyston, north east of Glasgow, on 4th July 1964. The engine was Perth-allocated under BR and survived to near the end of steam. Photograph by Sid Rickard from the J&J Collection courtesy Rail Photoprints.

SHANKEND – NO. 61937
South of Hawick, Gresley K3 no.
61937 has a Carlisle to Edinburgh
freight, mainly consisting of tankers,
at Shankend on 8th April 1952.
Photograph courtesy Rail Photoprints.

Above SALTCOATS – NO. 44820

A Motherwell to Largs excursion is south of Ardrossan at Saltcoats on 15th June 1963. Stanier Class 5 no. 44820 heads the train. Photograph by Sid Rickard from the J&J Collection courtesy Rail Photoprints.

Below SANQUHAR – NO. 42746

Hughes 'Crab' Class no. 42746 has a down freight south of Sanquhar (north of Dumfries) on 26th September 1961. Photograph by B.W.L. Brooksbank.

Above ST BOSWELLS SHED – NO. 64463

Located at the east side of St Boswells station, the locomotive shed was a stone-built two-track building completed by the NBR in June 1850 and was used for servicing purposes until 1959, later entering commercial use. Reid J35 Class 0-6-0 no. 64463 is outside the shed during 1954. The locomotive was erected by the NBLC in June 1906. By Nationalisation, no. 64463 was assigned to Hawick shed (St Boswells was a sub-shed of this) and remained the case to November 1959 when transferred to St Margaret's. The engine was sent for scrap in September 1960. Photograph courtesy Rail Photoprints.

Opposite ST BOSWELLS STATION – NO. 60152

On the Waverley route, St Boswells station was opened on 20th February 1849. Several names were used from this time to 1865 – Newton St Boswells, Newton Junction and St Boswells Newton – when St Boswells was settled on. A number of branches made junctions near St Boswells, including those to Reston, Kelso and Jedburgh. As a result, the station was substantial, consisting of a three-storey house, booking office, refreshment room and waiting room. Peppercorn A1 Class Pacific no. 60152 *Holyrood* has made a stop for water at St Boswells in January 1962. The engine had been in the Scottish Region from new in July 1949, mainly at Haymarket, though with short spells at Polmadie during the early 1950s. St Boswells station closed on 6th January 1969. Photograph from the Dave Cobbe Collection courtesy Rail Photoprints.

Above STIRLING STATION – NO. 60010
Gresley A4 Class no. 60010 *Dominion of Canada* is at Stirling station with the southbound 'Bon Accord' train in May 1964. The locomotive had a year left in traffic and was later preserved for display in Canada. Photograph by Revd J. David Benson courtesy A1 Steam Trust.

Opposite above STIRLING SHED – NO. 64520 AND NO. 8351
On 28th August 1948, Reid J35 Class no. 64520 and Reid J88 Class no. 8351 are in the yard at Stirling shed. Photograph by B.W.L. Brooksbank.

Opposite below STIRLING STATION – NO. 44998
The 16.14 train from Edinburgh to Callander has made a stop at Stirling station in May 1964. The engine is Stanier Class 5 no. 44998. Photograph by Revd J. David Benson courtesy A1 Steam Trust.

Above STIRLING STATION – NO. 62426

Opened by the Scottish Central Railway in 1848, the present station buildings at Stirling date from 1916 when a reconstruction project was completed under the Caledonian Railway. The NBR made connections with the CR line at Stirling from Alloa in the east and Aberfoyle and Balloch in the west. Ex-NBR Reid D30 'Scott' Class 4-4-0 no. 62426 *Cuddie Headrigg* has collected the Edinburgh-bound portion of the 12.00 Dundee to Glasgow train on 19th September 1957. Photograph by B.W.L. Brooksbank.

Opposite above STIRLING STATION – NO. 70036

In the early 1960s, the 'Britannia' Class Pacifics were concentrated on the London Midland Region, mainly at Crewe and Carlisle, with some at Holyhead. No. 70036 was a Carlisle Kingmoor engine from February 1964 to withdrawal in October 1966 after much of the earlier career had been spent in East Anglia, which was the original sphere of operation for the class. No. 70036 was named *Boadicea*, though in this image the plates have been removed. The locomotive has made a stop at Stirling station with a parcels train on 8th June 1965. Photograph by Revd J. David Benson courtesy A1 Steam Trust.

Opposite below STIRLING STATION – NO. 73148

The 10.00 train from Dundee to Glasgow pauses at Stirling station on 8th June 1965. BR Standard Class 5 no. 73148 is at the head of the train. One of the Caprotti-fitted class members, entry into service was made late in the steam era, March 1957. The engine was new to St Rollox depot from Derby Works and remained until condemned during September 1965. Photograph by Revd J. David Benson courtesy A1 Steam Trust.

Above STONEHAVEN – NO. 44799

A local service arrives at Stonehaven station on 27th July 1964. At the front of the train is Stanier Class 5 no. 44799 of Perth shed. Photograph courtesy Rail-Online.

Below STRANRAER SHED – NO. 73077

A scene in the yard at Stranraer shed captured on 7th September 1964. On the left is BR Standard Class 5 no. 73077, central is Stanier Class 5 no. 45126 and right is Stanier 'Jubilee' no. 45742 *Connaught*. Photograph by Hugh Ballantyne courtesy Rail Photoprints.

Above STRANRAER TOWN STATION – NO. 40920
A train for Glasgow waits to depart from Stranraer Town station on 3rd August 1956. Fowler 4P Compound 4-4-0 no. 40920 is employed and transferred recently to the nearby depot. Photograph by David Anderson courtesy Rail Photoprints.

Below STRANRAER TOWN STATION – NO. 41132
Fowler 4P Compound 4-4-0 no. 41132 has teamed with Stanier Class 5 no. 45432 on this local train from Stranraer Town to Glasgow on 3rd August 1956. Photograph by David Anderson courtesy Rail Photoprints.

Opposite above STRATHYRE – NO. 45468

The first section of the Callander & Oban Railway was opened for traffic in June 1870 and one of the stations on the line was Strathyre. Stanier Class 5 no. 45468 is pictured on 24th August 1960 departing northward with the 07.50 train from Glasgow to Oban. Class mate no. 45359 has been stopped to allow the train to pass whilst engaged on the Stirling to Oban daily goods train. Photograph by Hugh Ballantyne courtesy Rail Photoprints.

Opposite below STRAWFRANK JUNCTION – NO. 45121

An express freight approaches Strawfrank Junction behind Stanier Class 5 no. 45121 on 21st September 1963. The engine was amongst the last of a second batch of 50 Class 5s ordered from the Vulcan Foundry in June 1934 and was completed there in June 1935. New to Liverpool Edge Hill, by the end of the decade no. 45121 was recorded at Carlisle Upperby, then during the war at Inverness. At Nationalisation the locomotive worked from Motherwell and this continued to withdrawal in May 1964. Photograph by Sid Rickard from the J&J Collection courtesy Rail Photoprints.

Below STRAWFRANK JUNCTION – NO. 54461

South of Carstairs station, Strawfrank Junction was the point where the CR main line from Carlisle split to Glasgow and Edinburgh. The line to the latter (Strawfrank Fork) is curving away right in the background here, whilst the left-hand lines went to Carstairs station and Glasgow. The mechanical coaler belonging to Carstairs shed is also visible. Pickersgill 113 Class 4-4-0 no. 54461 is present as well, reversing into sidings with an engineer's train consisting of sleepers on 19th May 1957. This was in preparation for track work at Symington to the south. Photograph by David Anderson courtesy Rail Photoprints.

THORNTON JUNCTION – NO. 90444

A loaded coal train is at Thornton Junction behind WD 'Austerity' no. 90444 on 26th August 1965. Photograph by David Christie.

Above THORNTON JUNCTION SHED – NO. 65345
On 6th September 1966, Holmes Class J36 no. 65345 is in the yard at Thornton Junction shed. The engine's front numberplate has been removed and digits painted on the door instead. Photograph by David Christie.

Below THORNTON JUNCTION – NO. 90020
WD 'Austerity' no. 90020 has delivered a train to Thornton Yard on 6th September 1966 and is seen reversing back towards the depot (top left) for servicing. Photograph by David Christie.

Above THORNTON JUNCTION SHED – NO. 64618

Thornton was provided with a station in the September following the opening of the Edinburgh & Northern Railway in July 1848. At the aforementioned date a locomotive shed was built and the facilities were later upgraded by the NBR to a four-track depot in 1896. These were in use to the 1930s when the LNER demolished the depot and erected a new six-track shed on the branch to Dunfermline, west of Thornton Junction. A repair shop was included, along with a mechanical coaling plant and 70 ft turntable. Reid J37 Class no. 64618 stands in front of the coaler on 6th September 1966. The locomotive was a long-term servant at Thornton, though had just two months before condemned. Also seen is Gresley J38 no. 65901 which had a similar history, surviving slightly longer until April 1967. The shed closed at the same time and was later demolished. Photograph by David Christie.

Opposite above THANKERTON – NO. 72000

Around five miles south of Carstairs at Thankerton, BR Standard Class 6 'Clan' Pacific no. 72000 *Clan Buchanan* is northbound at speed with a Liverpool/Manchester express to Glasgow on 19th May 1960. The engine had recently transferred back to Polmadie depot after a six-month spell at St Margaret's. The aforementioned had been the locomotive's main residence, though another six months had been spent in the employment of Edinburgh Haymarket as duties for the class became increasingly scarce during the late 1950s. At Edinburgh the 'Clans' were generally used on Waverley route services, as well as some trains to Newcastle. No. 72000 was condemned at the end of 1962 after just 11 years in traffic. Photograph by David Anderson courtesy Rail Photoprints.

Opposite below THURSO SHED – NO. 54491

Being serviced in the yard at Thurso shed (built by the Sutherland & Caithness Railway in 1874) is Pickersgill 72 Class 4-4-0 no. 54491. Pictured in August 1960, the locomotive survived another year in the employment of Wick depot. No. 54491 had been there from 1953. Thurso shed was taken out of use in 1962. Photograph courtesy Rail-Online.

THORNTON JUNCTION – NO. 65920
A loaded coal train is coupled to Gresley J38 no. 65920
on 6th September 1966. Photograph by David Christie.

Above THURSO STATION – NO. 54491

Thurso station was the northern terminus for the Sutherland & Caithness Railway opened in 1874; operation was carried out by the Highland Railway. In August 1960, Pickersgill 72 Class 4-4-0 no. 54491 is at the station while surrounded by freight wagons. Photograph courtesy Rail-Online.

Below THURSO SHED – NO. 57585

Enginemen and McIntosh 812 Class 0-6-0 no. 57585 pose for the camera outside Thurso shed in the early to mid-1950s. Wick-allocated at the time, no. 57585 was condemned there in November 1961 following 61 years in traffic. Photograph courtesy Rail-Online.

Above THURSO STATION – NO. 40150

Sir Henry Fowler produced a 3P Class 2-6-2T design for suburban and local services in the early 1930s. Following Stanier's appointment, he perpetuated the type, with modifications, later in the decade and these numbered 139 examples. No. 40150 was amongst these and constructed at Derby Works in September 1937. The locomotive is pictured at Thurso station on 2nd May 1957. At the head of a local service, trains from Thurso and Wick were generally combined at Georgemas Junction and continued forward to Inverness. No. 40140 was allocated to Wick between June 1956 and August 1962. Photograph by Hugh Ballantyne courtesy Rail Photoprints.

Opposite above TROON, ARNOTT & YOUNG LTD SCRAPYARD – NO. 46155

As the Modernisation Plan intensified during the late 1950s, the number of withdrawn locomotives awaiting disposal at BR's main workshops grew immensely. The result was BR outsourced the task to private companies across the country. One was Arnott & Young Ltd, which had premises in Rotherham (near Sheffield), Glasgow and at Troon (north of Ayr). The first engines arrived at the latter location during 1959 and continued through to the end of steam. Fowler 'Royal Scot' 4-6-0 no. 46155 *The Lancer* is in an advanced state of deconstruction in Troon Yard on 9th April 1965. The locomotive had been condemned at Kingmoor in October 1964. The yellow diagonal warning stripe is present on the remaining cab side denoting restriction from the electrified lines south of Crewe. A tender is also being dismantled adjacent to the engine's remains. Photograph by R. Collen-Jones courtesy Rail Photoprints.

Opposite below THROSK – NO. 64623

South of Stirling, the CR made a junction to reach Alloa over the Firth of Forth via a swing bridge. This opened in 1885. In 1890 a platform was provided for the small settlement of Throsk, east of Fallin and a short distance from the bank of the Forth. During the First World War, a munitions factory was built nearby and a rail connection laid from the line. Reid J37 Class no. 64623 is pictured at Throsk in March 1963. Photograph courtesy Rail Photoprints.

Above WICK SHED – NO. 45170 AND NO. 4997
On 26th August 1949, two Stanier Class 5s are outside Wick shed. No. 45170 is left, with BR number and plate, whilst right no. 4997 retains the LMSR-style number and plate. Photograph courtesy Rail-Online.

Opposite WHITHORN STATION – NO. 57375
The 'Scottish Rambler No. 2' railtour took place over the Easter weekend of 1963. On the final day, 15th April, Drummond 294 'Jumbo' Class no. 57375 has reached Whithorn station on the Wigtownshire Railway branch from Newton Stewart. Photograph courtesy Rail Photoprints.

Below WICK SHED – NO. 44991 AND NO. 45124
Another pair of Stanier Class 5s are outside the depot at Wick, though in the 1950s here. Left is no. 44991 and right no. 45124; note the breakdown crane on the extreme left. Photograph courtesy Rail-Online.

BIBLIOGRAPHY

Allen, C.J. *Titled Trains of Great Britain*. 1983.

Baker, Allan C. *The Book of the Coronation Pacifics Mk 2*. 2010.

Barclay-Harvey, Sir Malcolm. *A History of the Great North of Scotland Railway*. 1998.

British Rail Main Line Gradient Profiles.

Dow, George. *The Story of the West Highland*. 1947.

Griffiths, Roger and Paul Smith. *The Directory of British Engine Sheds and Principal Locomotive Servicing Points: 2 North Midlands, Northern England and Scotland*. 2000.

Hooper, J. *The WD 'Austerity' 2-8-0: The BR Record*. 2010.

Hunt, David, John Jennison, Fred James and Bob Essery. *LMS Locomotive Profiles: No. 5 – The Mixed Traffic Class 5s Nos 5000-5224*. 2003.

Hunt, David, John Jennison, Fred James and Bob Essery. *LMS Locomotive Profiles: No. 6 – The Mixed Traffic Class 5s Nos 5225-5499 and 4658-4999*. 2004.

Hunt, David, John Jennison, Fred James and Bob Essery. *LMS Locomotive Profiles: No. 7 – The Mixed Traffic Class 5s Caprotti Valve Gear Engines and Class Summary*. 2006.

Hunt, David, John Jennison, Fred James and Bob Essery. *LMS Locomotive Profiles: No. 8 – The Class 8F 2-8-0s*. 2005.

Knox, Harry. *Haymarket Motive Power Depot, Edinburgh: 1842-2010*. 2011.

Larkin, Edgar. *An Illustrated History of British Railways' Workshops*. 2007.

Marshall, Peter. *The Railways of Dundee*. 1996.

Mullay, A.J. *Rail Centres: Edinburgh*. 1991.

Quick, Michael. *Railway Passenger Stations in Great Britain: A Chronology*. 2009.

RCTS. *A Detailed History of British Railways Standard Steam Locomotives: Volume One Background to Standardisation and the Pacific Classes*. 2007.

RCTS. *A Detailed History of British Railways Standard Steam Locomotives: Volume Two: The 4-6-0 and 2-6-0 Classes*. 2003.

RCTS. *A Detailed History of British Railways Standard Steam Locomotives: Volume Three: The Tank Engine Classes*. 2007.

RCTS. *A Detailed History of British Railways Standard Steam Locomotives: Volume Four The 9F 2-10-0 Class*. 2008.

RCTS. *Locomotives of the LNER - Parts 1 to 10A*.

Sixsmith, Ian. *The Book of the Royal Scots*. 2008.

Townsin, Ray. *The Jubilee 4-6-0s*. 2006.

Walmsley, Tony. *Shed by Shed Part Four: Scottish*. 2011.

Welch, Michael S. *Memories of Steam From Glasgow to Aberdeen*. 2002.

Yeadon, W.B. *Yeadon's Register of LNER Locomotives Volume One: Gresley A1 and A3 Classes*. 2001.

Yeadon, W.B. *Yeadon's Register of LNER Locomotives Volume Two: Gresley A4 and W1 Classes*. 2001.

Yeadon, W.B. *Yeadon's Register of LNER Locomotives Volume Three: Raven, Thompson & Peppercorn Pacifics*. 2001.

Yeadon, W.B. *Yeadon's Register of LNER Locomotives Volume Four: Gresley V2 and V4 Classes*. 2001.

Yeadon, W.B. *Yeadon's Register of LNER Locomotives Volume Six: Thompson B1*. 2001.

Yeadon, W.B. *Yeadon's Register of LNER Locomotives Volume Ten: Gresley D49 and J38 Classes*. 2001.

Yeadon, W.B. *Yeadon's Register of LNER Locomotives Volume Eighteen: Gresley K1 & K2, Thompson K1/1 & Peppercorn K1*. 2001.

Young, John and David Tyreman. *The Hughes and Stanier 2-6-0s*. 2009.

Also available from Great Northern

The Last Years of Yorkshire Steam

The Golden Age of Yorkshire Railways

Gresley's A3s

Peppercorn's Pacifics

London Midland Steam 1948-1966

The Last Years of North East Steam

British Railways Standard Pacifics

Western Steam 1948-1966

The Last Years of North West Steam

Gresley's V2s

Southern Steam 1948-1967

Yorkshire Steam 1948-1967

Gresley's A4s

Gresley's B17s

The Last Years of West Midlands Steam

East Midlands Steam 1950-1966

Thompson's B1s

The Glorious Years of the LNER

visit www.*greatnorthernbooks.co.uk* for details.